How to Keep
Being a Parent . . .

When Your Child Stops
Being a Child

How to Keep
Being a Parent . . .

When Your Child Stops
Being a Child

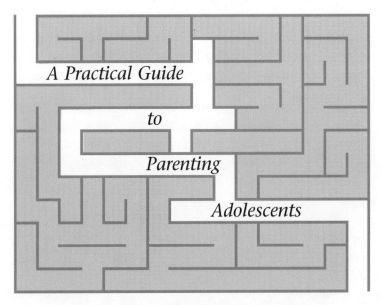

A Practical Guide

to

Parenting

Adolescents

Nic Cooper and Rick McCoy

WILLOW CREEK PUBLISHING
CANTON, MICHIGAN

Publisher's Cataloging-in-Publication
(Provided by Quality Books, Inc.)

Cooper, Nic.
    How to keep being a parent when your child stops being a child :
a practical guide to parenting adolescents / Nic Cooper, Rick McCoy.—
    1st ed.
    p. cm.
    LCCN: 99-68057
    ISBN: 0-9675426-0-X

    1. Parent and teenager. 2. Adolescent psychology. 3. Parenting.
I. McCoy, Rick. II. Title

HQ799.15.C66 1999   306.874
                                                    QBI99-1608

Interior design by Sans Serif, Inc. Saline, Michigan 48176

Illustrations by Kevin Franks

Printed in the United States of America by
McNaughton and Gunn, Inc., Saline, Michigan 48176

Dedication

With our deepest love and gratitude, we dedicate this book
to our parents, Ned and June Cooper and
Bob and Jean McCoy, who wrote our parenting manuals,
and to Nic's children, Angela and Sara,
and Rick's stepchildren, Jared and Meghan Nisch,
who have helped to refine them for us.

ACKNOWLEDGMENTS

We owe a great deal to a great many for their invaluable contributions to our own growth and thinking, upon which this book is based.

Two groups with whom we've shared a special connection and lasting friendship are the alternative education staff in Plymouth-Canton and the consultants who worked with us delivering PIPFest (Partners in Prevention) Weekend Retreats.

We have worked with hundreds of parents in a variety of situations. These parents often came into our lives with concerns about their teenagers. They also came, however, with a variety of skills that worked well for them. We are grateful to these parents not only for the insight which they provided us, but for the trust they placed in us when sharing their stories and accepting our help.

We also owe a great deal to Dale Yagiela, Scott Levely and the staff of Growth Works, Inc., an outpatient treatment center for adolescents in Plymouth, Michigan. It was here that we were able to learn about chemical dependence and its effects on families as we worked with both recovering adolescents and their parents. The courage and commitment demonstrated by these people on a daily basis continues to inspire us.

Ron Harrison, a social worker, and David Logan, a psychiatrist, both from Ann Arbor, were instrumental in teaching us how to approach the disease of chemical dependence assertively but with compassion. Their approach has helped literally hundreds of adolescents get straight and their families to get healthy.

Another figure who has been a valued inspiration and mentor in our careers is Earnie Larsen. His wisdom is found throughout this book. Earnie has written volumes about recovery for people either directly or indirectly impacted by the disease of chemical dependence. Reading Earnie's books, listening to his tapes or attending any of his workshops can be for others what it was for us—a life-changing experience.

We also wish to acknowledge those individuals who reviewed this book and provided valuable suggestions for making the final product more practical for our readers. These individuals are, first and foremost, loving and effective parents and include: Janet Early, a parent leader in the Plymouth-Canton (MI) school district; Mary Anne and Jim Eppley, long-time leaders and promoters of parent support groups; Pat Everett, parent coordinator for Saline (MI) schools; Dr. Steve Foley, a psychologist in private practice as well as for Plymouth-Canton schools; Judy Hodgkins, music teacher in Boston (MA); Sandi Jester, middle school teacher in Plymouth-Canton schools; Ginny Keelean, health occupations teacher for Howell (MI) schools; Dr. Becky Moore, elementary principal in Plymouth-Canton schools; Dr. Duane Moore, former superintendent of Wayne-Westland (MI) and South Lyon (MI) schools, currently a professor at Oakland University; Mark Schuby, a social worker in private practice and the Student Assistance Coordinator for Saline schools; Deb Shemansky, Student Assistance Program Coordinator for Walled Lake Western High School (MI); Sheila Pursglove, freelance writer and operator of a private child care center; Debbie Schopieray, an active member of several parent groups in Plymouth-Canton; and Dennis Williams, minister.

We conclude this list with the women who are first in

our hearts. We thank our wives, Jane Cooper and Sue McCoy, who have taught us their style of parenting and helped refine our own. They have been patient with the time we've spent developing and delivering workshops and refining this manuscript; supportive of our efforts; encouraging when we felt overwhelmed; and assertive in making certain that we kept our lives in perspective and didn't neglect our roles as husbands and fathers.

CONTENTS

PREFACE

We have each spent our entire careers working with troubled adolescents and their families. As we have struggled to assist these young people to discover their own strength and to become healthy, happy adults, several facts have become clear. One of the contradictions we have discovered is that while teenagers spend a great deal of energy challenging authority, they require it as much or more than any other time in their young lives. Stated simply: Although adolescents *defy* parents, they desperately *need* parents. Likewise, parents of adolescents also find themselves in conflict. How can we love our children so much and yet we sometimes find it so difficult to "like them"?

In our efforts to assist parents and their children through this difficult period of growth, we have offered a series of parenting workshops over the last several years. The response to these sessions has been universally positive, reinforcing another important truth: Parents of adolescents welcome help! Rarely have we encountered a parent wrestling with adolescent children who is willing to throw in the towel. Despite the frustrating behavior of the teenagers we have assisted, we consistently find their parents eager for helpful information and support.

It is for these parents that we have written this book. It is never too late to improve our parenting skills or to learn new strategies. On the other hand, *it is never too early to begin raising healthy teenagers*. Many times, parents who have participated in our workshops have come back to tell us how much these strategies have helped them with younger children, and many have expressed regret that they didn't have this information sooner. So while this book was first written for parents who have teenagers now, we also offer it to any parents who expect their children to become teenagers. (If you have children and *don't* expect them to become teenagers, you're definitely in for a shock!)

While the material in this book comes directly from our own experience and from the content of our workshops, we recognize that these ideas are certainly not new. Although our presentation of these concepts is completely our own, we have clearly been influenced by countless others in the field of human behavior. We have given credit where we have directly referred to someone else's material. We regret that we can never fully recognize all those whose ideas have contributed to our own.

Finally, when writing about adolescents, we often find ourselves laughing at their idiosyncrasies. We wish to assure our readers that even though we find their behavior undeniably humorous at times, we have a deep respect and love for those teens we have known and have yet to meet. We have chosen to spend our careers working with them and do so willingly and with enthusiasm. They are energetic, passionate, and ever-changing individuals. We laugh *with* them at their own inconsistencies, just as they laugh with us at ours!

This issue of respect is fundamental in dealing successfully with adolescents! Nic's daughters have reminded him often of how uncomfortable it is to hear people talk in negative terms about "teenagers". They are sensitive to jokes made at their expense which stereotype all teenagers as crazy or difficult.

Another parent provided a wonderful model of respect for teenagers when Nic was attending an open house at his daughter's middle school. Nic related a humorous moment from the previous day, when he found himself doing the "funky chicken" on Main Street in their hometown. The girl's father chuckled and said that this reminded him of an incident that occurred with his daughter. He looked directly at his daughter and asked her if this was all right to share with Mr. Cooper. She simply responded, "No." He assured her that this was okay and the matter was immediately dropped!

Nic found himself moderately frustrated, but since then, he has never shared personal experiences about his children in our workshops without their knowledge and approval. More than any other lesson we hope to teach in this book, we urge every parent to remember that despite those attitudes and behaviors which we find hilarious or infuriating, within each child lives the soul of a future adult, deserving to be treated with dignity and respect.

INTRODUCTION

Congratulations! Nobody parents their children perfectly. If you are reading this then you have already demonstrated your desire to parent more effectively, and your willingness to seek more information! This means you're a loving parent who wishes to help his or her children to become happy and successful adults. Strategies and techniques can be learned, but this basic attitude is critical and almost impossible to teach.

Perhaps more than any other human task, parenting is a highly personal experience. No two parents raise their children in exactly the same way. Nor is there any perfect way to parent. Like everything else we do, the way we relate with our children will always reflect our own personality and style. The last thing we would ever suggest is that everyone who reads this will parent in exactly the same way!

We are not offering you a set of recipes, but rather a set of tools. The theory behind "recipes" is that everyone will do exactly the same thing and will get exactly the same results. They make our life simpler because they allow us to bake just like the author. However, parenting is much more complex, and we all work with beautifully unique ingredients. No child is exactly like another. Even our own children are very different from each other.

In addition, each parent has his or her own personality and style. So, while some of you may have picked this up with the hope that you could simply follow a different set of recipes and get the same wonderful, predictable results, parenting will never be this simple.

This is why we prefer to think of the strategies we offer here as "tools". Although good tools increase our ability to do things, each of us uses them differently, according to our own personal style. As you use this guide, we encourage you to work through the exercises and try each of the "tools" that we suggest. Like anything new, you may find these tools awkward at first. This is only natural. Remember when you first learned to use "handwriting" instead of printing, or your first few experiences on a two-wheeled bicycle? Most of us found it awkward and unnatural at first. However, after practice, it became so natural for most of us that we now do it without thinking about it at all.

So go ahead and try these tools as you work through this book. Some may already be familiar to you. Others may feel awkward or unnatural at first, but stick with them...at least until you become a bit more comfortable with them. Over time, just as with handwriting or riding a bike, your own style will emerge, and you will use the tools in your own personal way.

The Nature of Adolescence

We believe the title we chose for this book summarizes our dilemma as parents. The problem with parenting teenagers is that we still need to be their parents, while they no longer view themselves, nor behave, like "children".

Certainly parenting is never an easy proposition at any age! Maybe the reason children don't become teenagers for twelve years is that parents need that much time and experience to get ready. While younger children cost us a great deal of sleep, anxiety, and energy, to be sure, they still tend to accept our authority more readily, and rarely presume that they can live without us.

With adolescence all this begins to change. Suddenly our children begin to think and act more like adults. No longer can we simply tell our children what to do or physically remove them from dangerous situations. At this age, they begin to challenge every form of authority. Even the simplest directions elicit open rebellion. Now we must develop a completely different type of relationship. This new relationship requires us to let go of some old strategies and understand adolescence more clearly. It's also helpful for us to think a little more about our own parenting styles and where we learned them. Since one of the greatest tools of all is knowledge, let's begin by taking a closer look at adolescence itself.

The Primary Tasks of Adolescence

Each stage of development has its own special job description. The primary job for an infant is to learn to move and to control his or her body. As children grow older, their primary tasks become the mastery of language, or social relationships. Likewise, there is a "developmental job description" for adolescents. In order for them to grow into healthy adults, they are now ready to take on two new tasks.

> **The primary tasks of adolescence require children to:**
> *(1) establish their own identities,* **and**
> *(2) assert their own independence.*

We often refer to independence and identity as the "two I's of adolescence". Before we look at tools for dealing effectively with adolescents, we need to understand these tasks and how they influence adolescent behavior.

Identity

Until adolescence, most of us find our identity in our family. We are content to be "one of the Smith boys", or "Mrs. Johnson's little girl, Sally". We identify with our parents and siblings, and accept this identity. But before we can take our place as an adult in the world, we must establish our own individual identity. It is our nature to move out and away from our biological family, and this requires that we define ourselves as unique individuals.

As our children go through the process of establishing and asserting their own individual identity, they begin to challenge our style and values, often "trying on" several new personalities in front of our eyes. Sometimes these changes come so quickly that they are almost humorous. At other times, this young stranger who shows up for dinner (or late for dinner) terrifies us. We need to remember that these trying times are exactly that: *"trying times"*. If we keep this in mind, we can avoid extreme reactions like total withdrawal or total control.

Let's look at another example. Imagine a husband waiting outside the fitting rooms while his wife tries on several new outfits. She emerges from the dressing room in a dress that he thinks looks ridiculous. He certainly doesn't run from the shop straight to a lawyer demanding a divorce because this isn't the woman he married! Nor, if he's wise, does he jump to his feet and forbid her to go out in public dressed like this. Why? Because he realizes that this is the purpose of this whole process, and feels valued to be invited to give feedback. She is only trying these things on, after all. No permanent purchase has been made. If he's a loving partner, he is interested in her own growth as well as that of their relationship. He offers his own opinion, stated in a manner considerate of her feelings, and respects the fact that the final choice will be hers. In this situation, he might say, "That's not the dress I would have picked out for you, but I love you for who you are more than for what you wear. It's your choice."

Likewise, when our adolescents "try on" new styles,

we need to remember that they are in that stage of development when it is natural and healthy for them to do this. We don't need to label ourselves as total failures, nor do we need to remain silent and walk on eggshells. It is our role to offer them our opinions, without engaging in all-out warfare. In this book, we will explore some specific tools such as "I-messages", valuing, modeling and listening, all of which can help us to communicate more effectively and maintain healthier relationships during these "trying times" of adolescence.

Independence

The other key task of adolescence is to assert one's independence. While we often ponder how to best raise our children, it's important to remember that we are really raising adults! (It's just that we *start* with children.) Think of the phrase "raising children" more closely. We are really "lifting" children, "growing" them so that they become mature adults. The last thing we want is for our children to remain totally dependent upon us for the rest of their lives! In order for them to complete the process of healthy growth, they must eventually separate from us and move out on their own. Although this is painful for all of us, both children and parents, it is absolutely necessary. So let's take a closer look at the process of achieving independence.

Transitional Independence

Young children are naturally dependent upon their parents and other adults to provide safety and structure. They actually take comfort from this dependence. However, as children become adolescents, they begin to strive for inde-

"Trying Times"

pendence. This new independence is one of the two "I's" that we discussed earlier. For most individuals (just like for many emerging nations), the process of becoming independent requires that at some point we defy what has been our prior authority. This process of defiance is natural and necessary, to a degree. This makes our children's' initial attempts at independent behavior awkward at best.

During this stage of "transitional independence", doing things "their own way" looks a lot like *JUST NOT DOING ANYTHING THEIR PARENT'S WAY.* It occurs approximately between the ages of 10 and 15 and takes on a different look with each adolescent. In some cases, our children challenge all rules and appearance norms. In other cases, they may find themselves compelled to argue about issues of importance like religion or family values. Whatever the battlefield, it puts an incredible stress on parents as we struggle to decide where to draw the line and how we should best respond to this behavior. Without a good deal of introspection and advance preparation, these conflicts can lead to some colossal confrontations which in some cases can cause lasting damage.

In order for parents to deal effectively and lovingly with this predictable period of defiance, we need to remember that this is a necessary function of the growing process, so we don't take these challenges so personally. This defiance of authority is only a stage in healthy development. Those individuals who are unable to move beyond defying all authority fail to achieve true maturity or healthy independence. So we also need to examine our parenting styles and personal values so that our reactions will be reasonable and loving. Our goal as parents is to guide our children *through* this period of transitional independence in such a way that they are able to move on toward healthy independence.

The Limitations of Adolescence

In addition to understanding these two primary tasks of adolescence, it also helps if we recognize some natural limitations. Developmental psychologists have observed that all adolescents share two significant limitations: (1) an inability to assess risks, and (2) an inability to conceptualize their own mortality. Let's look at each of these briefly.

High Risk Behavior

It probably comes as no surprise to parents of teenagers that they approach life with reckless abandon. As they strive to find their identity and defy authority in their efforts to be independent, they often choose activities that are intensely exciting and associated with risk.

We must remember, too, that one's ability to assess risk is based upon one's lifetime experience. The more mistakes we make, and the more consequences we experience, the greater our "database". We are better able to compare and to predict those activities or situations that hold a high degree of risk. We are also more motivated to avoid potentially painful consequences. But when we are young, we don't have as many life experiences to compare and have not yet suffered many painful results. This limits our ability to determine the relative level of risk inherent in situations we face.

Inability to Conceptualize Mortality

The other factor which probably contributes to such risk-taking behavior is the fact that children don't fully believe that they can be seriously hurt or die. This is not to suggest that they are unaware of world events, or that they are not exposed to death in our society. In fact, teenagers today are, regrettably, all too familiar with violence and death. It is a rare child who reaches the age of 12 today without losing an acquaintance to disease or violence. However, this limitation is one of attitude or belief. Although teenagers recognize intellectually that death is a reality, they consistently fail to accept at a gut level that it can happen to them.

Natural Outcomes

Once we understand that teenagers are compelled to assert their own independence and discover their own identity, while unable to grasp their own mortality and assess risks, many of their more discomforting behaviors become clear.

Taking Risks

In our workshops, we often have fun with parents designing a teenage "crest" or logo. We frequently agree that the symbol might well be the skateboard. How characteristic of adolescence to find great appeal in an activity which takes place at high speed, requires near-perfect balance and reaction time, and is practiced on cement! Then, when parents suggest a helmet or pads, kids look at us like *we* were crazy!

Adolescent children choose to engage in high-risk activities because of their inability to assess risk and to conceive of their own mortality. However, there may be additional factors which explain such behavior. A powerful way to assert one's independence is to do something which is forbidden, or at least discouraged. Also, in their effort to establish their own distinct identity, they will likely be attracted to activities which are unique from those of their parents. Physically demanding and risky behaviors fit the bill in each case.

Additionally, the chemicals released into the mind and body when a person is excited or frightened provide a "natural high" which has great appeal for young people. This may also explain the huge teenage market for frightening movies.

Peer Loyalty

One of the greatest frustrations we encounter in dealing with teenage children is their almost total disregard for our feelings or opinions, contrasted with an intense and almost blind loyalty to their friends. Nothing we have to offer seems of value, while anything that comes out of their friends' mouths seems to be law. This intense loyalty would be admirable if it weren't so exasperating!

When we remember the nature of adolescence, however, this becomes clearer. It's only natural that people leaving familiar territory would seek company. Isn't this what's really happening here? Forced by their nature to defy parents and the structure upon which they've come to rely, it makes sense that children would look around for others doing the same thing. Everyone also seeks validation when they have to take a risky position, and no one validates a teenager quite as unconditionally as another one.

A Preoccupation with Fairness

If the logo for adolescence is the skateboard, the motto would almost surely be . . . "It's not fair!" This battle cry issues forth thousands of times each day in homes with adolescents across the world. Why such a sudden demand for fairness?

Here again, the primary tasks and limitations of adolescence provide the clue. Young children rely on parents to protect them and their rights. Also, they tend to accept more readily the premise that right and wrong are clear and that the world is always fair. As they become more mature, however, they become more perceptive and realize that life is not such an absolute proposition. On top of this, they are about to strike out on their own. More than ever, they want assurance that the world is fair and predictable. Suddenly, they become highly aware of every slight and inequity.

Sibling Conflict

In our workshops, parents frequently ask why their teenagers are suddenly so hostile toward younger brothers and sisters. When we remember that their primary tasks are to assert their independence and identity, it makes sense that it would be easier to pull away from siblings than parents.

At this age, they desperately need their own space and individuality, and brothers and sisters are a nuisance. Also, in their zeal to demonstrate their new "maturity", they need to make it clear that they are no longer children and have nothing to do with children. Finally, as they define their own unique personality, they naturally focus on all the ways in which they are different from brothers and sisters. This frequently results in criticizing siblings mercilessly.

Family Conflict

Once we understand these primary tasks of adolescence, we should realize that periodic conflict is natural and healthy when we're dealing with adolescents. In fact, if you have teenagers in your home and are not encountering periodic conflict, something is probably wrong!

Loving parents have a huge emotional investment in their children. We know from experience that anytime people are forcibly separated from those they love, it causes us great pain. This means that as our children become more independent, as they should at this age, it is natural for us to struggle emotionally with this. It also means that when they overstep their limits, as we all do when we're learning new behaviors, we will have to hold them accountable. So take comfort! If there are regular conflicts in your home between you as the parent and your adolescent children, then you are on the right track. It's just that the track gets a little muddy here for awhile.

Although we haven't identified specific strategies for each of these behaviors yet, we hope that parents find some comfort in simply understanding that these are natural outcomes of the primary tasks and limitations of adolescence.

The Nature of Parenting

Although the way in which parents relate to their children changes when those children become adolescents, the five primary responsibilities of effective, loving parents remain the same. These are to provide:

1. a safe environment
2. consistent structure
3. support and encouragement
4. a clear set of values
5. an introduction to intimate relationships

We may at times grow weary of these responsibilities and complain that parenting feels like a one-way street. It is! While there are certainly countless rewarding moments as we watch our children grow, it is not healthy or reasonable to expect our children to provide any of these things for us. *We are the parents, they are the children.* This is an essential truth and one which is crucial to successful parenting and to our children's happiness.

A Safe Environment

Providing a safe environment is fundamental to healthy growth. A safe environment is free from abuse of any kind—physical, sexual, or emotional—and one in which a child can grow without fear of being shamed. The first part of this is pretty self-evident. We certainly don't need to elaborate on the devastating harm that abuse can cause a child.

Ironically, unless we deliberately develop other skills, we tend to repeat what was modeled for us by our own parents. No matter how many times you may have sworn to yourself that you would never treat anyone the way you were treated, parents who were victims of abuse as children are much more likely to become abusive parents themselves. So if you grew up with abuse, it is wise to seek the help of a good therapist to understand its impact upon you to prevent resorting to abusive behavior yourself.

In other cases, an abusive background does not lead to abusive behavior, but rather to a fear of all conflict in any form. For these individuals, the effect of an abusive background is that they avoid conflict at all costs. This can be just as damaging to an individual, and downright crippling to any adult who is trying to successfully parent an adolescent.

As we have already discussed, the very nature of adolescence involves a great deal of conflict. A parent who is unable to resolve conflict directly will be at a huge disadvantage in dealing effectively with their own teenagers. Of course, none of us particularly enjoys conflict. However, if you find that because of your own background, you are unable to handle conflict without hiding or resorting to violent behavior, then you must examine this issue and work on your own growth. This is essential in order for you to effectively respond to your own teenage children.

The second aspect of providing a safe environment is much more pervasive. This involves accepting mistakes without shaming the child. Shaming messages are words that say the child is bad like "you're just lazy", or "you'll never amount to anything", or "how could you be so stupid!" These comments do not address the child's behavior but assign negative characteristics to the child himself. No one deserves to be labeled negatively, but young adolescents are particularly vulnerable to these comments.

We have learned that the subconscious brain stores every single experience, including all those things that are said to us. When our parents, those whom we have listened to and valued the most in our lives, identify us in any way, we cannot help but store this as a part of our self-image. Frequently in counseling adults, we have heard middle-aged men and women repeat shaming labels, word for word, exactly as their parents stated them! Parents often make these comments when they are afraid, hurt, or frustrated. It is much better to acknowledge these feelings than to strike out at our children with a shaming statement. It is helpful to remember that "hurt people hurt people." It is appropriate for parents to openly acknowledge their hurt, but not appropriate or effective to hurt back.

We wish to make a clear distinction between "shame" and "guilt". Guilt is a healthy and appropriate consequence of unacceptable behavior. When we address children's inappropriate behavior, their discomfort is natural and the resulting feeling of "guilt" promotes healthy growth. Guilt is temporary and can be forgiven. In contrast, "shame" is not about the behavior, but is instead tied to a child's identity. Children don't walk away from shame. Instead, they incorporate it as a part of their self-image.

An adolescent who gets in trouble in school and feels

guilty about the behavior is experiencing the natural consequences. This guilt will help him to make a different decision the next time. If, however, his parents call him stupid, lazy, or dumb, he is shamed. These comments don't focus on his behavior, but on *him* and become a part of his developing identity.

Making mistakes is a natural part of life, and a significant part of adolescence! Therefore, the parent's role is to act as a guide when mistakes happen. One way to encourage growth is to ask, "What did you learn from this?" This approach allows us to turn a mistake into an opportunity for learning and is often much more effective than a lecture. This is not to say that we shouldn't give consequences. In fact, consequences are also an essential part of the learning process. Appropriate consequences allow us to help our children learn from their mistakes in a more controlled situation before they make choices which may have more disastrous results in the real world. We'll talk more about this in Chapter 4.

Consistent Structure

Parents provide structure by establishing clear boundaries and expectations. As we stated before, our children are not *our* source of support. We are there for them. An important part of providing structure is making that structure visible and predictable. It's essential that we make it clear exactly what behavior we expect, and what the consequences will be if these expectations are not met. Though our children will almost certainly resist this structure outwardly (remember it's a part of their job description to resist authority), especially when it limits their behavior, the truth is that they still take comfort from the safety and security which clear limitations provide.

In over twenty-five years of working with unhappy adolescents who were in trouble constantly, we heard many say, "I wish my parents would be parents." Often this was in reaction to the fact that they had unrestricted freedom. While they relished it outwardly, and even bragged about it to their peers, inside they felt "uncared for" because their parents did not restrict them from things that could be harmful. A lack of parental structure often results in *scared kids doing scary things*.

Support and Encouragement

The most powerful support we can receive is that of *unconditional love*. This is that very special parental kind of love that says, "I love you just the way you are, no matter what!" While this is easy to understand, it isn't always so easy to do. When children are younger, it's easier to accept their misbehavior as childish and to forgive it. We also tend to lavish more affection on younger children, maybe because they are somehow "cuter".

But when our teenage children make choices we find objectionable, it's harder to remember to separate the behavior from the child. When our child comes home with green hair, for instance, we may not be too excited about the new look, but we still need to love our kid. In this case, we can certainly express our feelings, but will probably accept this behavior as temporary. Loving our kids does *not* mean that we tolerate behaviors or choices that we see as dangerous, like cigarette smoking or body piercing. In fact, it is out of love that we set clear limits prohibiting harmful behaviors.

Perhaps the hardest time for parents of adolescents is when we begin to realize that our children are not fitting "our dream." Often, parents try to realize their own worth through the accomplishments of their children. When this is the case, children may begin to believe "I'm only as good as I do". This is the motto for an eventual "workaholic." Critical to avoiding this trap is to recognize your dream and let go of it when it is apparent that your child has other ideas. Then it is just as important to be supportive of their dreams. So what if your football player wants to be a ballet star? Love him all the way to the top—or to wherever he aspires!

A Clear Set of Values

While there is a lot of emphasis on how the media affects the values of our children, the fact remains that the primary responsibility for values education rests with parents. That is, if we do it! If we make our values explicit, clearly understood to our children, we can expect them to adopt them over time. It is true that they will likely examine and maybe even reject some of them. However, if we do not make our values clear, we are abdicating this responsibility. In that case, we are opening the door to "Beavis and Butthead", gangster rap or whatever else comes along.

One way to teach values is to state them openly. Tell your children why you choose to go to church or why you do not. If you abstain from alcohol, tell them why. If you do not, tell them why it is different for you or why it's OK for you.

Another more important way to establish values is to be congruent with your actions. If you value honesty, consider the message you send when your kids hear you tell your spouse to tell the person who is calling that you're not home. *Chicken Soup for the Soul* (first edition) includes an example of a father who understood this type of integrity.

> *It was a sunny Saturday afternoon in Oklahoma City. My friend and proud father Bobby Lewis was taking his two little boys to play miniature golf. He walked up to the fellow at the ticket counter and said, "How much is it to get in?"*
>
> *The young man replied, "$3.00 for you and $3.00 for any kid who is older than six. We let them in free if they are six or younger. How old are they?"*
>
> *Bobby replied, "Mikey's three and Johnny's seven, so I guess I owe you $6.00."*
>
> *The man at the ticket counter said, "Hey, Mister, did you just win the lottery or something? You could have saved yourself three bucks. You could have told me that the older one was six; I wouldn't have known the difference."*
>
> *Bobby replied, "Yes, that may be true, but the kids would have known the difference." (As told by Patricia Fripp)*

An Introduction to Intimate Relationships

Our first experiences with closeness and intimacy in relationships come from our experiences growing up in a family. The pleasure or pain we experience when we allow ourselves to care about and be vulnerable to others affects each of us deeply and often dictates the ease with which we are able to relate intimately to others for the rest of our lives. Those of us who grow up in close families whose members care about each other and are able to express feelings directly and safely are better equipped for intimate relationships of our own later in our lives.

In sad contrast to this, children who are not able to experience this level of trust and closeness as they are growing up are often unable to establish personally rewarding relationships as adults later in life. As parents, we need to encourage openness and the direct expression of feelings and needs in our children. We also need to allow ourselves to be open and direct about our own feelings, not only as an example for our children, but so that they can learn to be sensitive to the needs of others with whom they share a relationship.

Perhaps the most critical aspect of this type of intimacy is the ability to accept responsibility for our mistakes. This is how we undo those mistakes we make when we're hurt or angry. Nothing is quite as powerful to an adolescent child than hearing a parent say, "I'm sorry, I blew it." It heals things quickly and builds closeness. None of us are perfect. We all make statements that we wish we could take back. This is a powerful way to turn a parenting blunder into a positive experience. Often it is helpful to use our friends as a "sounding board" to help us maintain a healthy perspective. In some cases, we can turn to our own parents for counsel as well.

These, then, are the five primary responsibilities of loving parents. Our children require a safe environment, consistent structure, support and encouragement, a clear set of values, and an introduction to intimate relationships. In the next section, we will talk about the challenge of meeting these responsibilities in a variety of family structures.

Changing Family Patterns

Now that we've discussed what parents need to provide, it's time to recognize the realities of parenting in our current society. The truth is that fewer than 50% of all American families living together include both biological parents. This means that children are becoming adults within a variety of family structures. This presents an additional challenge to parents, but not an impossible one. We must remember that the five primary responsibilities which we have just discussed must be met, regardless of our family structure.

Solo Parenting

Perhaps the greatest pitfalls exist for the parent who is parenting solo! When one parent is removed from the team through death, desertion, divorce or a significant disability, the remaining parent must still meet these responsibilities. There are also cases in which two parents may reside in the household, but only one accepts responsibility for parenting. In any of these situations, it becomes much more difficult for a parent to keep things in perspective, without the benefit of a partner.

The daily stresses of everyday living weigh much more heavily on anyone trying to maintain a family alone. The temptation for solo parents is often to use children as a source of support or to make our children our "friends" when stresses become too great. This is inappropriate and potentially harmful to our children. *Children need friends* and *parents! We deprive them of the only parent they have when we try to make them our friends.* (While this is a powerful temptation for solo parents, no parent can afford to cross this boundary.)

We aren't suggesting that any one of us doesn't need support and perspective to parent children effectively. However, when we find ourselves confronted with the daunting task of parenting single-handedly, it becomes critical that we seek support and perspective from our peers! Unless we do, we will almost certainly be drawn into the unhealthy pattern of crossing boundaries and using our children for support and friendship. When we do, we not only confuse them about our relationship, but we rob them of the safety and structure which they count on us as parents to provide.

As soon as we begin to rely upon and "need" the support and friendship of our children, we can't help but weaken our position as their parent. Over the years in our counseling practice, we have often seen such relationships result in spoiled, controlling young adults. They learned that they can intimidate or control their single parents by threatening to withdraw their love or support if they don't get their way.

Separate Parenting

When divorced parents share the care of their children, other challenges present themselves. In amicable relationships in which both parents share similar values and don't wish to hurt each other, separate parenting can produce healthy adults. Openness is crucial to making this work, both with each other and with the kids.

Parenting problems abound, however, when the relationship between divorced parents is not a friendly one, as is often the case. In these situations, both parents need to remain adults and remember that *their divorce is from each other, and not from their children!* Regardless of their feelings about each other during and after their divorce, their children still rely on them as their parents. Such parenting arrangements work best when both parents understand and agree to support a clear set of expectations for their children. It is also critical that neither parent use his or her time with the children to "bad mouth" the other parent. To do so is to cross that healthy boundary we discussed earlier by using a child as a friend or for personal support. We must remind ourselves that the other parent is still their father or mother and they recognize that they are in some ways like this person. By attacking our ex, we are inadvertently threatening a part of our child.

Blended Parenting

"Blended families" provide parents with another particular set of problems. This structure, also becoming more and more common, creates a need for both parents to be open and honest with each other and with their new family. Each parent must slowly wade into their new role of father or mother, allowing for natural resistance to be expressed and acknowledged. What this structure provides, incidentally, is a powerful opportunity for lessons in intimate communication.

For some of us, the reality of parenting a child that is not "ours" is frightening. The best way to deal with this (as with anything else for that matter) is to be open about our feelings and needs. This does not mean that we ask the child to "fix" how we feel, but that we recognize and state our feelings as well as our intention to work hard at becoming a trustworthy parent. It also means assuring children that we do not intend to replace their natural parent, especially if there is still a healthy relationship there.

"Protective" Parenting

Sadly, some parents find themselves in a relationship with an abusive partner. This parent finds himself or herself regularly having to intercede, conspire with, or protect children from the harmful behavior of an abusive parent. When this happens, they are failing to meet the five primary responsibilities of parents. *Such parents owe it to themselves and their children to get help.* All too often, adults in abusive relationships tell themselves and others that they are staying in the relationship "for the children". In truth, remaining in such a relationship without getting help harms the children far more. Not only does such a relationship jeopardize children's physical and emotional safety, but it also creates a climate in which children learn to be abusers or passive victims. If couples are unable to end this behavior using outside help, it will be necessary to end the relationship.

When a relationship ends because of abuse, it may be necessary for a loving parent to deny the children access to the abusive parent. Doing this requires that we use the appropriate authorities and social agencies for support. In situations such as these, assuring our own safety as well as that of our children is critical to their healthy growth and development. When a parent is unable to act responsibly, then it is in the children's best interest to deny that parent's right to be with them. In these situations, the use of an outside therapist is frequently necessary to help the child to understand what is happening and to help the parent avoid being drawn back into an unhealthy relationship.

Our Parenting Manual

We often joke that children, like any other major investment, should come equipped with a manual. Ironically, given the importance of the task of parenting, it is one of the few responsibilities which is not yet regulated by a licensing board and requires no formal training or certification. However, it is our firm belief that parents do, in fact, have a parenting manual. Our parenting manual was written by our own parents, and contains the rules for parenting which they used to parent us! Without realizing it, we were memorizing our own parenting manual the whole time we were growing up. Earnie Larsen, a noted author and speaker in the field of alcoholism and codependence, said this with regard to learned, habitual behaviors:

> *What we live with we learn,*
> *What we learn we practice,*
> *What we practice we become. . . .*

The spoken and unspoken rules we grew up with, and the manner in which we were treated as children, dictate unconsciously the way in which most of us will treat our own children. Without even realizing it, most of us communicate expectations, reinforce behavior, and administer consequences for undesirable behavior in the same way our own parents did. In many cases, this is a positive thing. However, in other cases, we often end up repeating patterns which we found hurtful or ineffective when applied to us. The first step in changing our manuals is to recognize what is already printed there.

Family Rules

Everybody grows up with rules that govern their relationships within their family and set expectations for their behavior. Some of these rules are explicit, like "be in bed by 9 p.m.". Most of these family rules are never stated explicitly, but are clearly understood, and govern how family members communicate with each other. Recognizing these unspoken rules becomes particularly significant when we accept the challenge of parenting our own children, and especially when we begin facing the crises that occur during adolescence.

One of the areas in which we internalize "rules" is around the expression of feelings. The most healthy individuals among us are able to express a full range of emotions clearly and directly, without keeping them inside, or "stuffing" them. However, while growing up we may have experienced reactions to our feelings that gave us a different message.

For instance, if our parents responded to any expression of anger with rage, or by shaming us, it is likely that we learned to view anger as an unacceptable emotion. If we witnessed rage as the expression of anger, we may even see it as being dangerous and have learned to fear it under any circumstances. On the other hand, if anger was expressed directly by our parent(s), and if they were able to hear our own anger and respond with healthy concern, then we probably learned that anger was an acceptable and natural emotion.

In those instances where anger was not tolerated, the rule that children internalize is that "Anger is bad." Those of us who grew up with this family rule, and who fail to recognize or address this as adults, may avoid conflict and any anger-provoking situations altogether. Others may overreact to anger by quickly taking all the power in a way which will only inhibit positive communication.

We learn about expressing other emotions in a similar fashion. In the following worksheet, there is an opportunity to examine how your family of origin expressed the feelings of anger, hurt, fear, sadness, joy and embarrassment. To use this worksheet it is helpful to consider the following questions:

Was there a reaction that told you to avoid expressing that feeling?

Was it acceptable for you to cry? Shout? Be excited? Be afraid?

What was said or done that gave you the messages you got about these emotions?

By understanding how these feelings were expressed or prohibited in your family, you can come to better understand how you promote or discourage the expression of these feelings with your own children. This is particularly important with adolescents, where at times it appears everything occurs at a "crisis" level and emotions frequently become intense.

Another area in which to examine "family rules" is how they relate to specific issues. This first worksheet also asks you to examine the ways your family of origin viewed issues like conflict, time together, honesty, openness, mistakes and showing affection. These issues are critical to our children's healthy development of self-worth and integrity.

Of particular note are the issues of honesty, openness, and mistakes. In some cases, our parents may have verbalized a belief that honesty was important, but failed to demonstrate honesty in their own behavior. By now, most of us realize that we learn much more from example than from what is stated. In families where there is a chronic source of stress (what many authors call dysfunctional families), family members often conspire to deny painful issues, saying that a drunk parent is actually sick or a neglectful parent had something unavoidable come up. If we grew up in a family which was in denial about important issues, we will have difficulty being open and honest as parents ourselves unless or until we are able to identify and address these issues for ourselves.

The way in which parents respond to mistakes is equally critical. If mistakes led to shaming comments when we were children, we will likely repeat this behavior. On the other hand, if we are able to reframe our orientation to mistakes, and can accept mistakes as a necessary part of the learning experience, we can use them to teach and encourage our children without shaming them.

Now, take a moment and work on the first worksheet, reflecting on your family of origin. It is best to do this separate from your spouse or parenting partner, then compare your answers with each other noting how they affect you now. Remember also that this is not an exercise in "blaming." If your reflections uncover incidents that were difficult, remember that your parents parented in the only way they could, using *their* parenting manual.

∽✌

Parenting Manual—Worksheet #1

THE ORIGIN OF THE RULES

Describe the responses you got when you expressed the following feelings:

Anger

Joy

Sadness

Fear

Hurt

Shame

What were your family's expectations in each of these areas?

Conflict

Time together

Honesty

Talking about "real" issues

Making mistakes

Expressing affection

Based upon what you learned about how these feelings and issues were handled in your family of origin, you can now explore the underlying rule that governed this behavior. These rules are generally simple, like "anger is bad" or "tell people how you feel", etc. To discover the underlying rule, examine the reaction to the feelings or issue and ask:

If we asked your parents about how anger (or any other feeling) should be handled, what would they say?

Likewise, if we asked them for their beliefs about conflict, time together, honesty, etc. what would they say?

Do these responses describe your experience? If so, they are the rules that you've learned. If not, the "true" rules will be more easily uncovered by comparing what your parents *said* with what they *did*.

WORKSHEET NOTES

Parenting Manual—Worksheet #2

THE RULES

What were the rules about expressing each of the following feelings in your family?

Anger

Joy

Sadness

Fear

Hurt

Shame

What were your family of origin's beliefs about:

Conflict

Time together

Honesty

Talking about "real" issues

Making mistakes

Expressing affection

Our family of origin also teaches us what a father and mother "should be." In this case, by observing and listening to our parents we formed an opinion of how we "should" be when we assumed those roles.

We also experienced how our parents handled our transition to becoming independent. Their reaction undoubtedly had an impact on how we feel about our own children becoming independent. Some of us relish the idea, while others experience great discomfort as our children start to push away. Understanding the origin of our feelings about our children's independence will help us to approach it a little more calmly.

WORKSHEET NOTES

Parenting Manual—Worksheet #3

THE ROLES OF PARENTS

What did you learn about a Dad's role from your family of origin?

What did you learn about a Mom's role from your family of origin?

Describe how your parents felt about you becoming independent. How did they react?

Where along the continuum of growth pictured below are you most comfortable having your children?

Dependent |_____| *Independent*

Why?

WORKSHEET NOTES

After examining how your family of origin handled these feelings and issues, the next step is to assess the way you handle them now. This is the focus of the next worksheet. We recommend that you do this exercise with your spouse or significant other if there is another adult involved in the parenting of your children. This is also not a "blaming" or "finger pointing" exercise, but an opportunity to recognize what you have learned and what you may need to unlearn. In other words, be direct with each other and open to feedback but also gentle. Remember *you* do things the way you do them now because it is *the way you were taught to do them!* The best news about learned behaviors, however, is that they can also be "unlearned".

WORKSHEET NOTES

✥

Parenting Manual—Worksheet #4

YOUR RULES

Describe how you respond when the following feelings are expressed:

Anger

Joy

Sadness

Fear

Hurt

Shame

What are your own beliefs in relation to:

Conflict

Time together

Honesty

Talking about "real" issues

Making mistakes

Expressing affection

Now that you are more aware of the content of your own parenting manual, you can make some deliberate choices about what you wish to keep and what you would prefer to replace. What are the "rules" you wish to teach your children?

Take a look at the final worksheet now and see how your new rules compare with those we suggest for healthy families. If there is a significant discrepancy, we suggest that you discuss this with someone you trust outside of your family (e.g. a counselor, clergy, etc.) to be certain that these rules are good for you and your family.

WORKSHEET NOTES

❧

Parenting Manual—Worksheet #5

RULES FOR HEALTHY FAMILIES

These rules are ones that lend themselves to the healthy expression of feelings and can be used as a model for your family:

Anger—Anger is OK. It needs to be expressed promptly so it doesn't fester and grow.

Joy—It is important to express joy and happiness and it needs to be appreciated by others.

Sadness—Being sad is natural in times of loss or hurt. Crying is OK for everyone.

Fear—Fear is natural too. Everyone experiences it and no one needs to deny it. Courage is going forward in spite of fear.

Hurt—We all feel hurt sometimes. It needs to be communicated directly to those who hurt us to keep us from hurting back.

Shame—Shame is never OK. Guilt is natural but shame is destructive and needs to be avoided.

Conflict—Conflict is normal, natural and growth producing.

Time together—Families need to spend time together to appreciate each other. Quality time = quantity time.

Honesty—Honesty is not conditional. We need to be honest all the time, not just when it is convenient.

Talking about "real" issues—Healthy families talk about "real" issues. Secrets keep people sick.

Making mistakes—Mistakes are natural and a part of the growth process. They should be treated as learning experiences.

Expressing affection—It is OK to express affection to each other. It is also OK to choose not to openly express affection if that causes discomfort.

A Word about "Dysfunctional" Families

Many noted psychologists and authors in the field of codependence use the term "dysfunctional" to describe families impacted by alcoholism, abuse or other unhealthy behaviors. While these families certainly do not function ideally, they do function. We believe that the point is not so much the dysfunction itself, but what affects a family's ability to function.

The term dysfunctional may cause people who grew up in these families to feel additional shame when the fact is that their families probably did function as well as they could under the circumstances. In fact, if one of the functions of a family is to raise adults, then those whom we often hear stating that they "grew up in a dysfunctional family" only demonstrate that their family did in fact function to some degree.

The value of this term becomes even more questionable in view of the fact that some therapists have estimated that "98% of all families are dysfunctional at one time or another". (It is our belief that the other 2% are in denial.) This doesn't mean that families affected by alcoholism or other significant sources of stress don't react in a manner that contributes to unhealthy development. They often do. Several years ago, Claudia Black and Sharon Wegscheider, noted authors in the area of dysfunctional families, described family roles that are so consistent that it is possible to diagnose the presence of a chronic source of stress (stressor) just by hearing the descriptions of the various family members.

A more accurate focus, however, is not on whether the family functions or not but on the fact that there is a chronic stressor that creates compulsive reactions that may continue into adult life when the source of the stress is long past. Being aware of these behaviors is crucial to healthy parenting. It is also crucial that none of us feel ashamed about things that were outside of our control. For this reason, we choose to describe these "dysfunctional" families as "chronically stressed" families. The truth is that growth and survival in these families is very functional within their own context. What's important to understand is that the attitudes and behaviors that children learn growing up in chronically stressed families do not serve them well as adults when they make the transition to the greater community.

Tools For Healthy Relationships

How do we go about meeting the five primary responsibilities of parents? There are specific tools we can use that allow us to build positive parenting relationships with our adolescent children. These five tools are: listening, valuing, modeling, expressing feelings, and letting go. When we become comfortable using these tools, we demonstrate respect for our children, help them build a positive identity and become healthy, independent adults.

Listening

When Rick asks students why they need to listen, they can all tell him that they listen for information, but this is only half of the answer! What we often fail to learn, and to teach, is that we listen for *two* important reasons. Although it's true that the majority of the information we learn during our lifetime comes by way of listening, it is also the most powerful way to demonstrate that we value and respect another person. In a variety of surveys, when people were asked to identify what they valued most about spouses, parents, friends, and employers, the most common answer was the same: "They listen to me!" We all know how hurt we feel when others don't listen to us. It makes us feel that we are not important or worth their time.

Not only does listening to our children show them that we love and value them, but it also increases the likelihood that they will, in turn, listen to us! Listening, like other important elements in healthy relationships, takes time.

In addition to time, there are certainly a number of other obstacles to effective listening. Many times we find ourselves so eager to give advice, or to offer solutions, that we merely use the time when someone else is speaking to prepare our own answer. What we need to learn to do is to simply listen! This simple act of giving our children our undivided attention and really listening to their experiences, thoughts, and feelings tells them that we value them.

Often, just the opportunity to express our thoughts and feelings provides the clarity we need to solve our own problems. As young adults, our children don't always need to have us "fix" their problems for them any longer; they just need to know that we care enough to listen. Because these listening skills can go far to improve interpersonal relationships, you may find the letters of the word **FAR** will help you to remember the three skills: **F**ocus, **A**sk, and **R**espect. Let's look more closely at these key listening skills.

Focus

Effective listening requires us to focus our full attention on the speaker. Sure, we can hear without completely focusing on the source, but we can't demonstrate our respect for someone this way. We have probably all been frustrated by someone who has assured us, despite their newspaper, television program, or rock music that "I'm listening." In an important relationship, this isn't enough. We need to know that we have each other's full attention to feel valued. Does this mean that we must drop what we're doing every time our son or daughter wishes to talk with us? Of course not. But it does mean that rather than ignoring them or asking them to settle for our divided attention, we would be wiser to schedule a time when we can be fully attentive. A respectful response might sound something like this: "I'm really interested in what happened at school, but can't stop just now. Could we talk about this right after dinner?"

Ask Questions

Thoughtful questions show us that people are really listening, challenge us to reflect more deeply on our feelings and experiences, and improve our thinking and speaking skills. So why don't we ask questions? The most common obstacle is the fear of appearing ignorant. What a tragedy! When we don't ask questions, we lie to the speaker, by letting him or her believe we understand something that we don't! We fiercely protect our right to remain ignorant—the one thing we are trying to avoid! So ask! When we ask a question, we let the speaker know that we are really listening and that we want to understand. We affirm their knowledge, and we increase our own.

As parents, it's equally important to remember the difference between lecturing and listening. Our questions should be designed to open communication, not as thinly disguised lectures. We need to avoid rhetorical questions, no matter how hard it is at times. Questions like: "What were you thinking when you did that?" or "Didn't you know you couldn't get away with that?" or "Why would you say a thing like that?" are not really questions at all. They're simply judgments hiding in front of question marks. Better questions might be: "What else could you have done?" or "What would you do differently next time?"

Respect

Regardless of the message, it is critical that we respect the speaker. If we let our own frustration or adult judgment interfere with our support of our children, we have lost an opportunity to enhance our relationship. As parents we sometimes trivialize our adolescent child's concerns because our life experience tells us that what seems like a "huge" problem now will be insignificant tomorrow. Doing this, however, fails to show them respect by negating the fact that in *their* life experience this really is a significant problem and deserves our attention and respect.

You may use the following worksheet as a tool to examine your listening skills more closely.

~❧

Listening Worksheet

Exercise #1:

Monitor your interactions with your adolescent child for one day. How much of your communication with them involved:

Giving directions   _____ minutes

Lecturing   _____ minutes

Listening "politely"   _____ minutes   (listening with no
                                              interaction or recall of
                                              what was said)

Other types of communication
    (specify:_____) _____ minutes

Listening effectively   _____ minutes   (you know what they
                                              said, their perspective,
                                              and they left feeling
                                              valued)

Exercise #2:

In the next week, make it a point to learn three new things about your adolescent child by using good listening skills (focusing on them, asking questions about what *they* are talking about, and showing them respect). Write down the things you learned below. Also write down what you learned about your ability to listen.

What I learned:

What I learned about my listening (when is it easy?, when is it hard?):

Valuing

Another behavior which serves to enhance and maintain healthy relationships with children, or with anyone else for that matter, is that of explicitly valuing them. Of course we value our children, but many of us slip into doing this invisibly. We forget to make it clear, out loud, that we value them.

Authors have filled popular self-help books and magazine articles about relationships with reminders to tell others that we love them . . . yet many of us still presume that our loved ones know. We need to make it a practice to express our love often and tangibly. We often ask parents to remember when they were first in love. Most of us express our love frequently during this stage of a relationship . . . in notes, with flowers or gifts, and of course, verbally. With time, however, we begin to assume that those we love know it or we simply forget to tell them often enough. Probably no single act nourishes our relationship with our children more than taking time to tell them how important they are to us on a regular basis.

When we talk about valuing our children explicitly, we need to distinguish between "praise" and "encouragement". While praising another's accomplishments serves to reinforce desirable behaviors, it's *conditional*. In other words, praise is tied to a person's behavior, not to the person.

Encouragement, an important form of valuing, is a more powerful form of "unconditional" love. We need to let our children know regularly that we love them, *regardless* of their behavior. Since parents often find themselves trying to teach appropriate behavior, we more often tend to praise, but forget that what is even more important is our expression of love for *who they are*, not just for *what they do*.

Valuing, then, focuses on who our children are, not what they do. Just as shaming communication says negative things about what a child is ("you're lazy", "you're stupid", etc.,), valuing communication relates to the positive characteristics they exhibit. Think about how much more meaningful it is to hear, "Jamie, you are really a hard worker!" instead of, "Jamie, I'm really proud of you for getting that A."

Other examples of valuing statements include:

"When I see how you treat Tim, I see what a good friend you are."

"I really appreciate how trustworthy you are."

"It takes a lot of courage to do what you just did."

These statements become positive labels by which our children define themselves. Nic recalls a seventh grade basketball coach who frequently used him as an example of someone who "hustles." The effect that this pronouncement had on Nic was that he never stopped when he was on the court because he was a "hustler".

You may use the following worksheet to discover the positive qualities your son or daughter possesses and how you can share these with them. It also will help you to understand how it feels to do this.

∽❧

Valuing Worksheet

EXERCISE #1:

Observe your child for a week and make a record of positive character-istics that he/she exhibits. Also reflect on past experience to expand your list. Sometimes negative situations also illustrate positive charac-teristics such as independent thinking, persistence, etc. Doing this will help you to re-focus your attention in a positive direction.

Positive characteristics my son/daughter exhibits:

EXERCISE #2:

Now, when the opportunity presents itself, make valuing comments to your child, labeling positive characteristics that he or she is demonstrating right then. Be careful not to include an editorial comment such as "You are really a hard worker. *It's just too bad you can't work that hard at school."* (That will pretty much undo any positive feeling resulting from the previous comment.) Record your feelings and your child's reaction. Finally, record what you learned.

What I felt giving a valuing comment:

How my child reacted:

What I learned from doing this:

Modeling

No matter what we *say* to our children, we teach far more by our example! Young people are constantly watching adults to learn adult behavior, and they become increasingly observant as they become aware that they are approaching adulthood themselves. They may not listen to what we say, but we can be sure that they watch everything we do. In fact, we have probably all been embarrassed, as the following story demonstrates, by our own less-than-model behavior in front of our children.

> *One scorching August evening, a large family was gathered about the dinner table at a family reunion. The hostess turned proudly to her six-year-old daughter and asked if she'd like to say grace before the meal. Nervously, her daughter looked up and asked, "Mother, what do I say?" Her mother quickly coached her, "Oh, you can just say something you've heard daddy or me say, honey." Confident now, she lowered her head reverently and intoned, "Dear God, why did I invite all these people here on such a hot, hot day!"*

So the first part of healthy modeling is obvious. If we wish to raise healthy, moral children who behave well, we need to be healthy, moral adults who behave well ourselves! In this way, our children can provide us with a very useful standard for our own behavior. We would probably all be our best selves if we asked ourselves this simple question before each action: How would I act if my child was watching me?

However modeling is more than just being a good example. Teaching by example also requires that we call attention to the specific elements of healthy behavior. Many of us have watched someone demonstrate something, but failed to notice the right part or specific behaviors that insure success. We cannot safely assume that our children will always see the important parts of healthy behavior. They cannot, for example, see our thought process, and may not notice those things we do quickly and automatically.

Modeling means not only behaving well, but also *making the key ingredients in our behavior explicit.* This can be done simply, without turning every example into a lecture. It just means talking about our behaviors so that our children can better see what we're doing. As successful adults, we have learned a variety of life skills that we probably practice without much conscious thought and expect our children to learn from our example. But have we ever actually pointed these things out explicitly? We need to look for opportunities to point out those things we do that we want them to learn. This list might include:

- goal-setting,
- budgeting,
- managing our time,
- selecting friends,
- resolving conflicts, etc.

For example, we might take a moment to say to our son or daughter,

> *"I don't know if I've ever showed you this or not, but I take a few moments at the beginning of each month to set personal goals for the coming month.*

I've found that this keeps me focused and makes me more effective in my job. "

Another example might be:

"You know John is a good friend of mine. What makes him a good friend is that he's always stood by me, even in tough times, and even more importantly, I can count on him to be honest with me. He doesn't hide uncomfortable things from me that I need to know. "

A key aspect of modeling is resisting the urge to pressure your children to do things your way. In other words, explaining how and why you do something can be most powerful when you state it and let it go at that, allowing them to make a choice about trying this behavior themselves. (Some behaviors, such as the use of alcohol or other drugs, are obvious exceptions to this. For reasons that are probably clear, allowing an adolescent to make such choices is dangerous and irresponsible. We'll address this more in Chapter 6.)

The next worksheet helps you identify behaviors you would like to model and provides an opportunity to practice modeling them for your son or daughter. Incidentally, don't be discouraged if your son or daughter doesn't overwhelm you with his/her response. Trust that your message is getting through even if the result isn't immediately apparent.

∾

Modeling Worksheet

EXERCISE #1:

Reflect on some processes, values or other things you have learned and would like to share with your children. List these below, as well as the reasons you practice or believe them. This may include anything from budgeting to picking friends to religious beliefs, etc.

Things I'd like my children to learn:

Why these are important to me:

EXERCISE #2:

At an appropriate time, demonstrate to your child how you do one of the above things or speak with him or her about why you believe the way you do. Be careful to follow this with listening and not with a lecture about why she or he should do or believe as you do. Record your feelings as well as your child's reaction and your own insights from this experience.

How it felt to model:

How my child reacted:

What I learned from doing this (what was easy, what was hard):

Expressing Feelings

People are feelings-driven creatures. As teachers, it has been humbling to realize that most behaviors result from feelings more than from knowledge. This doesn't mean that knowledge isn't valuable, or that we don't draw upon prior experience and knowledge in making decisions. It just means that our emotions play a powerful part in directing our behavior. The following diagram illustrates the way in which this seems to work.

Experiences > Feelings > Impulses > (Conscious Thought) > Behavior

In response to each of our experiences, we have feelings. Everything that happens to us makes us feel happy, sad, hurt, afraid, ashamed, angry, or some other shading or combination of feelings. Though we may not be consciously aware of our feelings at the time, they trigger impulses to behave in a certain way. We have no control over the feelings or impulses which we experience. They are an automatic human response to our experiences, and we all experience them.

However, we have the capacity to apply the process of conscious thought to our behavior. This process requires us to take time to think, and to be aware of our own feelings and impulses. Small children, and those adults who are not able to apply this rational process, behave "impulsively". Their behavior stems directly from their feelings and impulses without benefit of rational thought. In order to behave responsibly, we must learn not only to resist impulsive behavior, but also to recognize, accept, and express our feelings directly.

Because many of our feelings are painful, we often use

what psychologists call defenses. These are mechanisms which allow us to avoid experiencing painful feelings. Although these defenses are natural, and allow us to survive intensely painful feelings until we can deal with them effectively, they can become an obstacle to healthy behavior and intimate relationships. When we habitually refuse to recognize our own feelings by employing these defenses, we fail to realize what is driving our behavior. We also lose the ability to be vulnerable to others. When this happens, we are no longer capable of enjoying or maintaining close personal relationships.

Earlier we said that one of the important functions of parents is to introduce children to intimate relationships. This requires that we teach our children that feelings, though they may be painful, are normal and need to be expressed directly. The best place to begin, of course, is by expressing our own feelings clearly and directly to our children.

There have been several models developed for expressing feelings directly. These are often called "I-Messages", because they are about "me", rather than "you". The point of an "I-Message" is to express our own feelings directly and clearly, without accusation. The model which we find most effective includes these five critical parts:

I Care . . . I See . . . I Feel . . . I Need . . . I Will . . .

Let's look at each of these important parts, one at a time.

We begin by letting people know that we care about them. This not only motivates them to listen, but more importantly, it reminds us how important they are to us, and that we don't wish to hurt or attack them. Here are some examples of the "I care" element of an "I" message:

"Cindy, I love you and you are very important to me."

"I care about you, John, very much."

Next, we describe the *specific* behavior which has triggered our feelings. This is the I "see" element. This isn't an opinion or a judgment, just a specific description of a behavior. Here are some examples of this element:

"When you come in at 1:15 and your curfew was 12:30. . . .

"When you roll your eyes at me and turn your head when I'm talking. . . .

In the third part, we express our feelings directly. Again, this isn't an opinion or judgment, just a statement of feeling. It's important to use a feeling word here such as mad, sad, happy, hurt, ashamed, afraid, etc. It is also important to note that if we follow the word "feel" with words like "that" or "like", we are *not* stating a feeling, but really a thought or opinion. This is usually a veiled judgment. "I feel *that* you are being inconsiderate," includes no feeling word and really means that we are judging someone's behavior. Here are some examples of the "I feel" element:

"I feel scared and angry."

"I feel hurt."

This is followed by letting them know what we need from them. This statement clearly expresses our own need in the relationship without shaming or blaming the other person. It should be a very *specific* statement. Here are some examples of the "I need" element:

> *"I need you to call if you are going to be late, no matter what the reason."*

> *"I need you to wear a watch so you can keep track of the time."*

Finally the statement concludes with the "I will" element, which is simply our commitment to them. This statement allows them to know *specifically* what we will do in the future. It is not intended to be used as a threat but may state logical consequences if the behavior isn't corrected. Here are some examples of the "I will" element:

> *"I will listen to your explanation and take it into account."*

> *"I will not ground you automatically if you're late, if you've called in advance when something unforeseen occurs."*

> *"If you are unable to make your curfew and don't call, I will need to make an earlier curfew."*

In this manner, we can express our feelings directly and clearly, without lecturing or attacking.

Let's be perfectly clear at this point. The reason we need to express our feelings is to model healthy behavior, and address our own needs in an intimate relationship. It is not to shame the listener into new behavior. In other words, we don't tell our son we feel hurt by his behavior so that he will apologize. We do it so that we don't store up that hurt until it turns to resentment or anger, resulting in inappropriate behavior on our own part. We do it so that he can learn how healthy adults express feelings in a direct and respectful manner. (When a father communicates this way, a child learns that it's perfectly normal and natural for a man to feel hurt.) Sure, we hope that when he knows how his behavior impacts others, he will take a closer look at it, but that is not our primary purpose.

While this formula may well seem artificial or cumbersome at first, remember that every new behavior, from a golf swing to riding a two-wheeler, seemed unnatural and awkward at first. Stick with it! Over time, this formula will become much more natural, and will go a long way toward healthy relationships . . . not just with teenagers, but with spouses, friends, and business associates as well. Listen to the difference between an accusatory statement and an I-Message, based upon this formula.

> Accusatory: *"That's it! This is the last time you're coming in so late mister! Don't you ever think of anyone but yourself?! You're not only grounded for the next week, but you can just kiss the car good-by until I think you're ready to be responsible!"*
>
> Direct: *(using an I-message) "I love you, son. When you come in after curfew and haven't called home, I feel hurt, afraid and angry. I need to know that I can trust you to be home on time, and that you'll call if you have to be late for some reason. I'll expect you to be home on time after this, and I will move your curfew up if you come in late again."*

The first approach is judgmental and hurtful. It's a product of our own feelings and impulses, rather than a rational statement of our feelings and needs. In addition, it will likely only trigger resentment and a defensive response. The second example doesn't sound rigid or stiff, but includes all five parts of the I-Message and is much more "hearable". Notice that there are still consequences and clear expectations, but they are stated directly and without turning this into a personal attack. Incidentally, while it is best if the "I-Message" isn't screamed, it can be delivered with feeling.

The next worksheet gives you an opportunity to construct an I-Message first in an artificial situation, then in one that is real to you. Remember, this will be awkward and takes practice to feel natural.

❧

I-Message Worksheet

EXERCISE #1:

Construct an I-message for the following situation:

Your child leaves the living room a mess after having some friends over after school. When you come home from work, you encounter this mess and are expecting guests for dinner. Your child has left with these friends and left a note indicating that he or she will return in time for dinner.

I care _____

_____

I see _____

_____

I feel _____

_____

I need _____

_____

I will _____

_____

EXERCISE #2:

The next time your child does something that frustrates you or makes you angry, respond to them using the I-message format.

Describe the situation:

Write an I-message that will best communicate your feelings and needs:

Describe the result of using this message and what you learned:

Letting Go

Maybe the most difficult, yet most empowering strategy for enhancing our relationship with our adolescent children is knowing when to let go. As we stated earlier, we often say that parents raise children when what we really mean to say is that we are raising adults. We are merely starting with children. If we're really committed to helping our children become adults, then at some point it will be necessary for us to let go.

When Rick was a teenager, he was invited to go waterskiing with some more experienced friends. At one point, he realized that his skis were too loose, and tried to signal for the boat to take him in. Instead, the boat sped up and as the toes of his skis caught in the wake, both skis were instantly left behind. In his panic, he tried to retain control by fiercely clutching to the tow rope . . . only to be dragged along and smashed into the water at high speed. Reflecting on this incident, it seems to teach a valuable lesson about letting go. We only get hurt when we hang on and try to control those things over which we ultimately have no control. If we would learn to let go, we would certainly reduce our own suffering, with no real loss of impact.

Put another way, we believe that strong parents are much like booster rockets. It is our job to provide sufficient direction and support, or "thrust", to get each of our children "launched" on their own life paths. It is also our job to know when that job is done and to let go! Obviously, timing here is critical. If we let go too early, we fail to provide sufficient direction or support, and are neglectful as parents. If, on the other hand, we hang on too long, we become an additional burden and hold our children back, prolonging their dependence upon us . . . and incidentally getting "burned" by their own booster rockets.

It feels good to know we are needed and it's difficult to let go of those we love, but it's perhaps the most important part of parenting.

Simple Doesn't Mean Easy

Even though many of the principles we discuss here may be relatively "simple" to understand, they certainly aren't "easy" to apply. Parenting small children requires a tremendous amount of physical energy. But just when we survive our children's' early childhood and think we can finally slow down a bit, we discover that parenting adolescents requires a great deal of *emotional* energy.

This requires us as loving parents to be sensitive not only to the needs of our children, but to our own needs as well! Because dealing effectively with teenagers is so demanding, we must learn to respect our own limits.

Members of Alcoholics Anonymous have thousands of phrases and acronyms which help them to practice the principles through which they maintain sobriety and enhance the quality of their lives. One of these is the word HALT. The letters of the word "halt" remind them that they are most vulnerable to relapse when they are *H*ungry, *A*ngry, *L*onely, or *T*ired. Surely this device has equal value for parents of adolescents. We would be wise to remember our own limitations, and avoid confrontations when we are stressed. While there are a few confrontations that demand immediate attention, we need to take care of ourselves and resist being "stampeded" into a confrontation before we are ready to deal with it effectively.

Discipline— Structuring Healthy Growth

To fully understand discipline, let's start with the word itself. It comes from the Latin word *discere* which means "to teach." This is the real purpose of discipline. It teaches, not punishes. Discipline for adolescents is essential as they become more independent and focused on building a positive identity. Everything we do as parents must be done with these two questions in mind:

> *How will this teach them to become more independent?*
>
> *How will this help them build a more positive identity?*

This means that the two strategies critical to effective discipline are to teach and affirm our children at every opportunity. When we address behavior that is inappropriate, we must teach them why it is a problem and what is expected. These *lessons* must be specific and filled with examples. They must also be delivered without shame or sarcasm.. When we do this we are giving our children a road map to appropriate behavior and an understanding of why it's essential.

Regular affirmation is equally important. We affirm our children when we identify the positive choices they make. Doing this requires that we be attentive to small changes. It also requires that we stop with the affirmation and resist the temptation to mention any irresponsible behavior.

Key Principles of Effective Discipline

If we wish to help our children through this difficult period of adolescence and keep discipline in perspective, we must understand and accept a basic truth.

> **Our choices and behaviors are a direct reflection of our own self-image!**

It is our contention that every choice a person makes is based upon his or her own self- image. If we see ourselves as competent and worthwhile, our performance and choices reflect this. If we see ourselves as incompetent and of little value, we will make decisions which reflect this as well. This principle applies in every area of our life.

Watching his wife apply make-up one day, Rick jokingly suggested that she could just apply it flawlessly to the mirror one time, and save a great deal of time on following mornings. All she would need to do would be to line her face up and she would appear ready for the day! Obviously, such a suggestion is foolish! Changing the reflection doesn't do anything to the source.

This has clear implications for the manner in which we address our children's decisions and behavior. If we try to micromanage their behavior, or dictate their decisions, we may meet with some limited, short-term success, but we're really only changing the reflection. In fact, by exercising this kind of external control, we send the subtle message that we don't believe they are capable of handling this issue by themselves. In this way, we may actually reduce their own self-image, with negative long-term consequences.

If we examine our own life experiences, we will find this to be true. When we feel capable and competent, we make better choices and are more effective in everything we do. When we see ourselves as incapable, no matter what our friends or family try to tell us, we are not apt to take risks or to be very successful.

This is not a new truth! We have probably all heard statements like: "Birds of a feather flock together." or "Water always seeks its own level." when we were growing up. These old sayings were merely another way of recognizing the same principle. We all choose friends and situations which reflect the way we see ourselves. This isn't to say that peer influence isn't a powerful force on all of us, but we need to remember that our children, like ourselves, *choose their peers*. Therefore, if we wish to support our children in making healthy choices, we can best do so by helping them view themselves as strong, competent individuals.

This key principle also helps us to remember that our teenagers' behavior is *not* a reflection of us! To the extent that we treat our adolescents' behavior as a reflection of us, we not only take on a lot of unnecessary embarrassment and shame, but we also find ourselves trying to control their behavior for the sake of our own image or reputation! In so doing, we actually send the message that they are not capable, and end up undermining their self-image in direct contradiction to this key principle. Certainly we should do everything in our power to help them learn to make good choices, but we must accept that when they fail at this, the consequences are theirs, not ours.

To do this we must learn to separate the child from the behavior. Earlier we discussed ways of communicating and suggested addressing behavior directly instead of making shaming statements that demean the child. When an adolescent makes a mistake, we can be most effective if we focus on the behavior or the choice that was made and stress the consequences of this choice. We need to avoid statements that label the child as bad or incompetent. These would be statements like "I can never trust you!" or "You're a liar". The alternative, which keeps the focus on the behavior, is to say "You didn't tell me the truth in that situation" or "You didn't do what you said you were doing last night." By separating the behavior from the child, we retain the role of teacher or guide rather than that of a critic. (Sadly, the world will provide more than enough critics, but we can never have enough supporters.)

Obstacles to Effective Discipline

There are several obstacles that interfere with our ability to discipline effectively. Many of these have to do with our own personal histories. In that respect, it might be helpful to refer back to the "parenting manual" that we discussed and completed earlier. For most of us, the three main obstacles to effective discipline are:

- our own "hot buttons",
- our tolerance for conflict, and
- our ability to avoid the "shaming/blaming" trap.

"Hot Buttons"

When we speak of our "hot buttons", we are referring to those particular issues which trigger an intense emotional reaction in us when they occur. This happens for a variety of reasons. First, there is what we refer to as the "loss of the dream." This is the realization that our child may not be the athlete/cheerleader/musician/actor/etc. that we hoped. When this appears to be the case, our disappointment sometimes triggers a more powerful reaction than is appropriate.

Another potential "hot button" for each of us is any behavior which violates those values to which we are most strongly committed. For example, if we feel that honesty is a fundamental value and the basis of all relationships, we may find ourselves particularly outraged when we must deal with a child's dishonesty.

Finally, and probably the most powerful of all our

"hot buttons", are those behaviors that recall feelings or events from our own childhood. These are specific behaviors that trigger our own childhood memories in such a way that they make us children all over again, experiencing all the intense feelings we felt when we were younger.

Imagine yourself expressing your anger to your son or daughter, while they react by smiling, laughing or rolling their eyes. While this is a common way for teenagers to defend themselves in such a situation, it may take on additional power if we encountered adults who did not take us seriously when we were angry as children. If this was an especially sensitive issue for us, our children's repetition of this reaction may well cause us to relive those old feelings. Suddenly we find ourselves responding not only to our son or daughter, but to all those adults who never valued our feelings in the way we felt they should. In situations like these, we are more likely to become irrational and less effective!

When we are dealing with "hot buttons", it's important to remember that it's not the button but what it's wired to! Consider the button that operates an elevator and the button that detonates a nuclear bomb. Both look pretty much the same, but pressing each one causes a dramatically different reaction! Similarly, each of our "hot buttons" are wired to distinctly different personal experiences. When we understand this and can understand why our reaction is so intense, we can gain better control over it. With an adolescent who may be trying to find our buttons for whatever reason, our own understanding of these hot buttons can go a long way toward diffusing them and help us maintain control of situations before they become ugly.

Tolerance for Conflict

The second obstacle to effective discipline can be our level of tolerance for conflict. Once again, as with most things, the seeds for this were probably sown in our own family of origin. If family conflicts were heated and frightening for us as children, we will likely attempt to avoid them at all costs. Conversely, if conflict never happened (at least visibly) in our home, we may avoid it at all costs because of the instinctive fear that it must somehow be dangerous or bad.

Examining the way conflict was handled in our own family will help us better understand our own reaction to conflict when it occurs in our lives now. As we said earlier, conflict is absolutely unavoidable when we are dealing with adolescents. Therefore, it's important to understand that conflict is normal, natural and healthy. It is not only normal, but is often the catalyst for growth. We need to learn to embrace it as normal and acceptable, and let it work in a positive manner. By re-framing conflict this way, it will be easier to accept it when it appears.

The Shaming/Blaming Trap

Finally, the "shaming/blaming" trap is yet another obstacle to discipline with its roots in our background. Remember that *shame is the number one growth inhibitor!* We often tend to use it through sarcasm and in the belief that it will motivate our children to change. In reality, shaming only hurts! It is also a telltale sign of our own hurt or fear. Many of us shame others when we are desperate to change their behavior. We shame when we are angry. Another fundamental truth is that *anger is almost always tied to either hurt or fear.* If you remember this, you will have a better handle on how to respond when your adolescent's behavior (or anyone else's, for that matter) makes you angry. If we recognize the core feeling that someone's behavior is eliciting in us, we can avoid the impulsive response of "hurting back" and remember our purpose in discipline.

Blaming is another self-defeating reaction to our children's choices. When we blame others, we actually hold our children *less* responsible for their own choices. This, in turn, gives them less control and decreases their independence. If we really want to support their healthy growth, we need to hold them accountable for their behavior. Then we can encourage them to examine their behavior and learn how to make a better decision the next time they find themselves in a similar circumstance.

We have often encountered students who are adept at getting parents and teachers to blame each other for the student's poor performance. In other cases, teenagers have learned to play one parent against another. In any case, when the adults allow themselves to be drawn into such a position and begin to blame each other, the outcome is disastrous. Ultimately, the only person who really has control over the outcome, the teenager, is relieved of responsibility while the adults engage each other in battle.

The following worksheet is designed to help you explore your background and discover your own obstacles to effective discipline. Take a few minutes to complete this worksheet, reflecting on your past as well as current beliefs. It is best to complete this worksheet individually at first, and then discuss the insights you gained with your partner.

Obstacles to Effective Discipline

What is the ideal behavior/attitude I wish to teach my child(ren)?

What is my own personal "hot button"? (What behavior or attitude most disturbs me?)

Why is this particular behavior/attitude so powerful for me? Where does this issue originate for me? (specific memory, event, situation, saying, etc.)

What type of discipline was I exposed to as a child? What were its benefits? What were the costs?

What are my greatest fears about disciplining my child(ren)?

What do I believe good discipline is and how have my own experiences as a child influenced my beliefs?

The Effective
Discipline Model

Remembering that the goal of discipline is to promote independence and a positive self-image, there is a simple continuum that can help us to make decisions about appropriate disciplinary responses. The continuum, pictured on the next page, consists of two parallel lines. The top line represents the range of behavior from irresponsibility or dependence to responsibility or independence. This line represents the behavior that an adolescent child exhibits in various settings. Below it is another line ranging from maximum structure on one end to minimal structure on the other. This line represents the range of parental responses. Simply stated, a child's position on the top line should dictate the parent's response along the bottom line.

Let's look more closely at the top line. When a child (of any age!) behaves irresponsibly, such behavior requires someone else to accept responsibility and therefore makes him or her more dependent on external structure. On the other end of the spectrum, responsible behavior leads to greater independence. The bottom line in this model simply suggests that the amount of external structure which a parent must provide should reflect the degree to which the child is behaving responsibly.

FIGURE 1: EFFECTIVE DISCIPLINE MODEL

Irresponsibility/   Responsibility/
Dependence   Independence

___ x _____ y ___

Adolescent Child's Behavior

Maximum   Minimum
Structure   Structure

___ x _____ y ___

Parental Response

In this model, "x" behavior elicits "x" parental response. For example, the adolescent stays out too late on more than one occasion. The parental response may be more structure. Initially, the parent may have given the child responsibility to be in at a reasonable hour. This apparently was not sufficient structure, so increased structure will mean setting a definite time limit. "Be in at 11:30 p.m." Then if the child does not comply, specific consequences related to being trustworthy about time may be imposed. "Grounding" may be a logical consequence for this behavior.

In contrast, "y" behavior elicits "y" parental response. In this case, the adolescent comes in by an acceptable time without any specific direction from the parent other than to be in at a reasonable time. In this situation, the "y" parental response requires no additional structure since the adolescent is acting independently. An appropriate parental response would be to acknowledge and affirm this as independent and trustworthy behavior.

To use this model, think of a behavior in which an adolescent engages. For example, let's imagine a child who comes home from school every day and immediately gets started on homework. This behavior would fall toward the responsible/independent end of the continuum. Such behavior clearly requires less structure from the parents. This child is already acting independently and needs no external structure to encourage this behavior. Therefore, the parent in this case will not need to set a "homework time" or monitor the child's work. This would only be overlooking what is already healthy, independent behavior.

Instead, the respectful parent would do well to respond by identifying and affirming their child's independent behavior. This teaches them that this is the desired behavior and affirms them for engaging in it. Remember by "valuing" the child and naming this characteristic, we increase the likelihood that he or she will engage in it again and apply this quality in other settings.

In contrast, imagine an adolescent that is not being so responsible (this one probably isn't too hard for many of us). For example, this adolescent is given the instruction to be in at a reasonable time. This expectation gives the adolescent the opportunity to act responsibly and to be independent. Instead, however, this adolescent comes in after midnight, a time which his parents do not consider reasonable.

The next step is to assert greater structure. Obviously, this child needs a clearer definition of the term "reasonable". So, in this case, the parent sets a time for him to arrive home. Let's say in this case that the time is 11:00 p.m. Unfortunately, however, this child fails to take this seriously and believes that midnight is early enough. So when he returns at midnight, the parent addresses this again. On the first occasion, it may be necessary to just explain why this is an important rule and also establish a consequence if he is unable to adhere to it. Then if there is another occasion, the consequence is enforced exactly as it was stated.

The consequence should reflect the behavior. It should, wherever possible, be a natural consequence of the behavior. For example, if being irresponsible in adhering to an agreed-upon curfew is the problematic behavior, it's only logical to restrict their ability to go out to the next planned social event. This "grounding" should be short-term to be effective. When we "ground" children for a week, month or more, it loses its logic and also denies them the opportunity to indicate they can be responsible.

In addition, the effectiveness of an undesired consequence is in proportion to the impact it has on the child. It has been our experience that adolescents are wonderfully adaptive, and quickly learn other ways to entertain themselves, or else begin to make our own lives miserable when they are grounded for extended periods of time.

In the example above, the parent responded to each successive, irresponsible behavior with increased structure. Each time the adolescent was given the opportunity to be responsible and chose not to be, the structure increased a little. At each of these points, a wise parent takes the opportunity to teach the adolescent what is expected and label desirable behavior as "independent". "When you come in at the appointed time without us having to monitor it, then we will see that you are being independent and will be able to relax and trust you more." We always need to state our expectations clearly and point out the fact that with responsible behavior comes greater independence.

In our parenting workshops, we offer participants a one-page summary of essential discipline strategies. We have included a copy of that handout in Appendix D.

Expectations

In some cases, parents fail to make their expectations clear. While we may react when our expectations are not met, we may have failed to make them clear at the outset. To avoid this, take time with your spouse, significant other or a supportive adult to identify your expectations for your child at home, at school and with friends. After writing down what it is that you expect, check to see if you have made these expectations clear to your child. If all they hear is "don't do that", they may not have a clear idea of what they *should* do! While we would never expect anyone to be successful at target-shooting with a blindfold, we are often guilty of essentially the same thing with our children. While our expectations may be obvious to us, we can never be too clear with our children.

Assessing Our Children's Behavior

All children are not created equal when it comes to developmental stages. Some will be very responsible from an early age and require very little intervention while others will test us all along the way. It is a common myth that parents must do the same things with each child. Although it's important to be consistent, consistency does not mean that we must always respond in exactly the same way. In our efforts to provide direction and our basic responsibilities discussed earlier(safety, support, structure, ethical values, and intimate communication) we will almost certainly be required to respond to each child differently.

We also need to remember that no child is equally responsible in all arenas of his or her life. Using the continuum introduced here, think about a particular child at home, at school and with friends. When we do this, we often find that the same child who may be irresponsible with regard to schoolwork is very mature in his or her selection of friends. We will also find that each of our children operates at a different level of responsibility.

This model provides us with a frame of reference that can help us clarify our responses when it becomes necessary to respond to one child differently than to another. The adolescent doctrine of "fairness" (see page 10) will present a challenge here. However, when we are able to be explicit about the behavior that the child is engaging in, and can clearly differentiate it from that of his or her siblings, as well as from the target behavior, we have a more solid foundation for our position and can demonstrate more easily why different consequences may be applied to different children.

❧

Assessing Your Children

HOME:

Dependence/
Irresponsibility

Independence/
Responsibility

|⎯⎯⎯⎯⎯⎯⎯⎯⎯⎯⎯⎯⎯⎯⎯⎯⎯⎯⎯⎯⎯|

SCHOOL:

Dependence/
Irresponsibility

Independence/
Responsibility

|⎯⎯⎯⎯⎯⎯⎯⎯⎯⎯⎯⎯⎯⎯⎯⎯⎯⎯⎯⎯⎯|

FRIENDS

Dependence/
Irresponsibility

Independence/
Responsibility

|⎯⎯⎯⎯⎯⎯⎯⎯⎯⎯⎯⎯⎯⎯⎯⎯⎯⎯⎯⎯⎯|

WORKSHEET NOTES

Selecting Consequences

We have already stated that the most effective consequences are those that are naturally linked to the behavior. When consequences follow naturally from inappropriate behavior, they not only make more sense, but they also keep attention focused on the particular behavior which created the problem. For example, if an adolescent child is spending too much time on the phone and not completing his or her schoolwork, a natural consequence is to restrict phone use. It doesn't make sense to ground the child for this behavior. On the other hand, if getting in late is the issue, not being allowed to go out is a logical consequence, because in this case the issue is trust.

As we have cautioned earlier, we recommend that parents be especially careful with grounding. It is generally only effective for short term use, such as one or two days. After that, the child adapts and the parent is the one who usually suffers the greater inconvenience . . . and the parent was never the problem!

Effective consequences are also the ones that affect things that *our children* value. Things like computer/Nintendo time, time with friends, phone usage (the adolescent umbilical), and ability to go shopping are of greater importance to them and things they would like to avoid losing. When these consequences are linked directly to the behavior, it meets the adolescent's "fairness" test and is likely to modify their behavior. A good strategy is to brainstorm with a spouse, significant other or support person a list of potential consequences in advance. This will help make disciplinary situations more dispassionate and effective when a crisis arises.

When considering consequences, there are a couple of other things to consider as well. First, remember the old phrase "nothing left to lose" and avoid putting yourself in the position of taking everything away! This type of response negatively affects the self-image that we want to promote. In fact, when everything is taken away, or consequences are too prolonged or severe, the adolescent often becomes so hurt and resentful that he or she loses all motivation. This rarely creates a climate which promotes healthy change.

Additionally, wise parents select consequences which are easily manageable. When consequences are complicated or difficult to enforce, they are almost certain to be applied inconsistently, and will be less effective. Not only will they be less effective, but our recollection of a painful situation does little to support future attempts to impose consequences.

Finally, parents would be well advised against restricting activities that are vital to our children's positive self-image. We are often asked if it is appropriate to prohibit participation in a sport or musical interest as a consequence for inappropriate behavior. We generally suggest that parents think hard before using these as a consequence or even threatening to use them. Such activities are critical in the support of a positive self-image and as this is one of the primary goals of parenting, it seems contradictory to take them away, especially in the case of a child who is already having difficulty.

The Home Contract

There are occasions when it seems that nothing is working or that the "fairness" principle has become overwhelming. At these times, it might be necessary to establish a "home contract." This document is *not* a contract such as one which exists between management and a labor union. It is merely an explicit statement of parental expectations as well as the consequences for failure to meet these expectations and the rewards for demonstrating growth. Such contracts have proven very useful when things appear to be getting out of control.

The form we provide is adapted from one used for adolescents returning home from chemical dependency treatment. In those situations, it is critical that expectations are understood and followed for the adolescent to survive or to stay in the home. In other situations, the use of a contract may be a last intervention before seeking outside help or a tool to structure behavior which may supplement outside help. Outside help may include therapy or police intervention if the behavior is dangerous or incorrigible. Remember natural consequences are an important element in the learning process. Better to allow our children to experience these now so they can learn from mistakes before the consequences are even greater. (In Chapter 6 we will discuss serious behavior problems like substance abuse where no disciplinary responses are likely to work. In these cases, loving parents *must* seek outside help.)

One final point about discipline in general and the home contract specifically is to remember the value of rewarding appropriate behavior. While we often associate terms like discipline and consequences with punishment, studies have consistently shown that in general, rewards do more to motivate desirable behavior than does punishment. These rewards do not have to be major, but we should recognize when our children do things well and show them that we appreciate their growth. These things enhance our relationship with our children, and help to "cement" the learning.

Home Contract (sample)

I, _____ understand the following expectations, rewards and consequences explained in this contract. I agree to abide by them and to directly express concerns that may arise from this contract in advance of a conflict.

FRIENDS:

Friends who will help me be successful and with whom I can have healthy fun are:_____

_____

_____

_____

I understand that being with these friends at appropriate times is encouraged as long as they continue being healthy for me.

Others that are obstacles to my success and are to be avoided are:

_____

_____

_____

_____

_____

Home Contract (continued)

SCHOOL SUCCESS:

To assure my school success, I will set aside the following time on the days indicated to study: _____

_____

_____

_____

I will ask for help when it is needed from: _____

_____

_____

My goal for my performance in school is to achieve:

_____

_____

_____

_____

The reward for achieving this goal will be:

_____

_____

_____

The consequence for not achieving this goal will be:

_____

_____

_____

Home Contract (continued)

HOME EXPECTATIONS:

I will do the following chores around the house within the designated timelines:

Chores: _____

_____

_____

_____

_____

Deadline for these chores to be completed:

_____

_____

The reward for completing these chores will be:

_____

_____

The consequence for not completing them will be:

_____

_____

CURFEW:

I will be home on weeknights by: _____

On weekends by: _____

Any changes in these times for special occasions will be decided in advance.

Home Contract *(continued)*

The reward for maintaining my curfew will be :

_____

_____

_____

The consequence for not maintaining my curfew will be:

_____

_____

_____

I also understand that the use of drugs, alcohol and cigarettes is prohibited and may be reason for obtaining a chemical dependency evaluation or for involving the police.

_____   _____
Adolescent's signature   Date

_____   _____
Mother's signature   Date

_____   _____
Father's signature   Date

Specific Areas of Concern

P arents frequently wrestle with certain common areas of concern. In this section, we will address three specific areas which many of us find difficult: school, friends, and sexuality. As we look more closely at each of the following areas of concern, we need to remember the key principle of behavior we introduced earlier, that "our choices and behaviors are a direct reflection of our own self-image." As we grapple with each of these specific problem areas with this principle in mind, we should constantly seek ways to raise our children's self-image with the knowledge that this, more than anything else, will ultimately result in improved behavior.

School Performance

Theories explaining student's poor school performance abound. "Experts" have assigned blame to everything from the state of our schools and the educational system, to the eroding American family, low reading skills, the media, drugs, poor nutrition, and rock music, to mention only the most common. While no one element is fully responsible, there is probably some truth in each and every theory.

One factor that is often overlooked is the fact that our society has experienced a very messy divorce in the last generation, and our children are suffering educationally. *This is not a divorce between parents, but the divorce between schools and homes.* Most adults over 40 today agree that when they were students, their parents were much more supportive of their schools and teachers. A discipline referral at school almost certainly meant that there would be consequences when you arrived home. Somewhere along the line, perhaps because of frustration with poor student performance, parents and teachers have begun to distrust each other. Too often, teachers blame parents for student problems, while parents blame the teachers. Sadly, as in many divorces, many children have gotten lost in this conflict, and have ceased to be held responsible for their own behavior.

Parents who wish to support successful school performance need to remember that, just like every other choice and behavior, their children's school performance will be a reflection of their own self-image. Children who feel good about themselves, and who believe that they are competent and capable, will behave this way in school.

In addition, we urge parents to work with school staff, rather than against them. Parents need to let the teachers and administrators know that they have high expectations for their children, and that they are willing to support their children's success in school. They need to listen to what school staff have to say and keep lines of communication open. Finally, it is important to apply each of the tools we discussed earlier.

Listen

Taking time to listen to our children's perspective on their school experiences without judging or lecturing can be a powerful tool. Just by showing an active interest in their feelings and attitudes about school, we demonstrate our concern without lecturing or trying to control their performance. This is more than just saying "how was school today?" It means listening and reflecting their feelings when they are sharing their experiences.

Often, our children come home from school with something to share, not uncommonly about some injustice they perceive. It is easy at these times to lecture, explain, or even scold as a way of straightening them out. However, it will lead to deeper conversations if we listen to the feelings being expressed and respond to them in a more reflective manner, which may be stated as simply as "you seem really upset." Listening and clarifying their ideas will lead to more sharing. Then, once we have established a non-judgmental interest, we can more effectively ask if they would like to hear our perspective. If they say they would, we have permission to give our viewpoint and it will probably be given more credence.

Value

It is also important to for us to remember to frequently identify those healthy habits and characteristics that we value in our children, especially those that relate to school performance. Identifying these positive qualities will go much further toward encouraging academic achievement than any amount of nagging or threatening. Some examples are "you're a very hard worker", "I like the way you solve problems", or "I really like the way you hang in when things get difficult." These types of valuing comments help them to recognize traits that will serve them well in school and help them to be more successful. They become part of their own identity as they approach new school situations.

Model

We must look for opportunities to point out those behaviors that help us to be successful in achieving our own goals. By explicitly highlighting our own work skills, we will not only demonstrate our personal commitment to hard work and achievement, but will also teach our children valuable skills to assist them in school. Examples include explaining:

> *"When I'm faced with a particularly difficult problem that I haven't faced before, I look for someone who is expert in that field and ask for help."*

> *"I have a major report due at work next week so I've divided it into five sections and plan to complete one each night giving me a couple nights to review and revise it."*

It is important when modeling to demonstrate the behavior and explain it at the same time. That gives the reason for the behavior while demonstrating how to apply it. Some of the best students we have encountered have clearly been influenced by parents, in many cases single parents, who have put themselves through college or returned for a high school diploma, while raising their children. Contrary to these parents' fears that their schoolwork robbed them of quality time with their children, their teenagers subsequent academic success only served to demonstrate the incredible value of modeling!

Express Your Feelings

It is also essential that parents feel free to express our feelings about our children's academic achievement and choices, just as we would in any other arena. When they make poor choices or fail to make their best effort, they need to know how we feel about it. (Remember of course that they also need to hear how we feel about their successes.)

Be clear and direct, without shaming or blaming.

> *"When I see that you are not completing work, I feel frustrated because you always say you've got everything done."*

> *"I'm happy that you've chosen to seek help on your own. That demonstrates maturity."*

> *"I feel scared when I see your grades falling because it could hurt you in the long run when you're applying to college."*

> *"I feel very excited that you've earned such high grades. Your hard work is paying off!"*

These comments express your feelings clearly without negative labels such as "lazy" and by focusing on the positive qualities demonstrated (asking for help shows maturity and earning high grades is a result of hard work) instead of just saying "good job."

Let Go

Ultimately, no one can make anyone else learn! Perhaps the most effective academic strategy for parents of teenagers is to leave performance in school up to the student. Think again about the primary tasks of adolescence—to establish an individual identity and to assert one's independence. At this age, it is far more important for most young adults to demonstrate that they control their own lives than to get good grades. In a world in which they still lack a great deal of control, school is one of the few areas in which they really are holding all the cards.

Dr. Julia Thomason, a noted educator and authority on middle school education, once wisely suggested that "if you don't want anyone to get your goat, you ought not to let them know where it's tied!" All too often, we have worked with bright, capable students who appear to be failing for no good reason . . . until we meet with their frustrated, angry parents. After talking with these parents, it becomes clear that their children have discovered that the quickest way to assert their own power is to defy their parents' need for school success. Frequently, when the same parents are able to step back and let their children take charge of their own academic achievement, things slowly turn around because the student can now be independent and still succeed in school.

Peer Relationships

Another issue which frequently arises is parental concern about unhealthy or undesirable friends. Here again, we need to remember the key principle that all choices are a reflection of an individual's self-image. Contrary to many parents' secret beliefs, the "wrong crowd" doesn't kidnap or hypnotize our children to become their friends. Young people *select* associates based upon how they see themselves, or at least how they wish to be seen.

Probably the two most common mistakes parents make in this area are attacking and/or forbidding certain friendships. Fierce loyalty to peers is one of the trademarks of adolescence. As soon as a teenager's friends are attacked, the "code" practically demands that they be defended. In fact, the tendency to defend that which is attacked is a basic human quality. As counselors, we have both learned that the quickest way to cement a client's commitment to a person or position is to criticize it. Although parents may disapprove of certain associates, criticizing or attacking them is almost certain to backfire.

Likewise, forbidding certain associations is usually unsuccessful. Not only does this challenge our children's independence, but it only makes that which is forbidden seem all the more appealing. This is also a universal response. If we think about it, it is the same for us too. Don't we "dig in" when someone forbids something we think we want? Criticizing or absolutely forbidding certain associations is rarely effective, primarily because it challenges the primary tasks of adolescence again. All this really does is to identify opportunities for our children to assert their own independence.

Are we saying then that parents should stand mute and watch their sons and daughters make poor choices? Of course not. To do so would be neglectful. So let's revisit the five tools again.

Listen

Rather than dictating or trying to manage our children's selection of friends, we would be more effective if we asked direct questions and listened to the answers. Often, the answers can provide some real comfort. One particular parent told us about his concerns when his son began to associate with another boy who was failing in school and whose appearance was frightening. He wore extremely long hair, leather jackets, and had poor personal hygiene. When this parent went home after one of our parenting sessions and asked his son directly why he chose to hang around with this young man, the answer surprised and comforted him. His son replied, "Dad, his parents are getting a divorce and he's all alone right now . . . besides, he's a great artist." By simply asking and listening, this father learned that his son was not trying to be tough, but rather was demonstrating sensitivity and an interest in art.

Value

"Choices are a reflection. . . . Choices are a reflection. . . . Choices are a reflection. . . . "

Every time we remind our children of their good qualities, we support these qualities that much more, and increase the likelihood that they will seek others with these same qualities. Trying to arrange or manage our children's peer relationships is like putting the make-up on the mirror. Instead, we need to focus our energy and attention on the process of supporting their best qualities, secure in the knowledge that their own self-image will eventually dictate their choice of friends.

Model

When was the last time, if ever, that we spoke openly about how we select our own friends? Have we ever explained exactly why we value those people with whom we choose to socialize? Making and maintaining healthy friendships, just like everything else, is a skill . . . and skills need to be taught. Remember once again to keep it simple. Modeling needn't become a major presentation complete with diagrams and overheads. It might be as simple as:

"Have you ever wondered why Jack and I have been friends for so long? Even though he makes those really corny jokes and gives me a hard time about my car, he's always been there for me during tough times. I guess one of the things I've always valued in our friendship is that he accepts me just the way I am and has stuck by me through good times and bad."

Express Your Feelings

As in other areas of our children's lives, we are allowed to have our own feelings and have a right to state them directly. In fact by now, they expect us to have these feelings. As long as we are respectful in the way we state them, we can be heard and our feelings can be valued.

"I love you and value your happiness. I've noticed lately that you seem to be spending a lot of your time with

Sarah. It seems to me that every time you disagree about where to go or what to do, you always end up giving in. This makes me sad. I need to know that my friends take my desires into consideration and I want the same for you. I support you in sticking up for yourself."

Let Go

In the area of friends, it is difficult at times to let go. We want to control because we want to protect our children from "bad influences." Again, it is critical to remember that our children are choosing these friends. So the focus might more appropriately be placed upon the reasons for their choices. Forbidding unhealthy friendships often leads to "underground" relationships. Instead, it is better to examine the *source* of the reflection and *let go* of the reflection itself.

There is one aspect to consider, however. If there is a history of misbehavior with a certain friend or friends, we may limit their contact with that friend to supervised situations. Even at this, it is important to understand that we are not with them at all times and if we don't clarify why we're concerned and listen to their perspective, our efforts are likely to be futile. So, in the end, do what you can to listen, value, model and express your feelings, then when it's all said and done, let go.

Emerging Sexuality

Sexuality is an issue that we often fear and sometimes avoid during our children's adolescence. Unfortunately, it is one issue that must be addressed if our children are going to develop into healthy adults. The media and today's culture are rife with sexual images and sexual comments. This makes it essential that we, as parents, assert our own values in a realistic and helpful manner. This is difficult for many reasons, the biggest of which is probably fear.

Common Obstacles to Healthy Discussion

One of the greatest obstacles to direct discussion for most parents seems to be our own discomfort with the topic of sexuality. Many of us grew up in a different culture—one in which sexuality was a more private issue. For us, as parents, direct questions can be discomforting or even embarrassing. However, most adolescents are no longer naive about this issue. In fact, by adolescence, they have already been instructed in the mechanics of sexuality through school programs, if not in the home, as well as the many health risks which attend sexual activity today. So introducing them to the "birds and bees" is no longer the focus at this age.

The critical issues for today's adolescents revolve more around the questions of when to become sexually involved and the implications that sexual involvement have for each of us. Many of us may simply wish that our children would wait until they were married because we realize the potential that sexual involvement has to interfere with young lives. Our discussion of this subject needs to be an open one, where we can clarify our concerns and freely respond to the many "whys" that our children are likely to ask.

To effectively address the topic of sexuality, it is helpful to first discuss it with our spouse or significant other to clarify our own feelings and position before we attempt to discuss this with our children. Having done this, it is critical that we treat the issue seriously when we undertake any discussion with our children. In some cases, parents (often dads, sorry) are inclined to make this a humorous issue. They may tell jokes or poke fun at alleged sexual behavior. Although this is probably a natural response to our own discomfort, we need to remember that *everything* we say carries a message. If we treat sexual behavior as something to be laughed about or in a manner that is not respectful, our children will learn to adopt this perspective.

When not laughing at it, parents who are afraid to address this issue may just decide to avoid it completely. In some instances, parents hope to handle this by leaving a particularly significant magazine article out in clear view, hoping that their son or daughter will approach them and say "hey, can we discuss this?" Who are we kidding? If we're too uncomfortable to initiate such a discussion directly, do we really think our adolescent is going to do so?

A third, and equally inappropriate manner in which parents sometimes decide to talk about sexual behavior is to engage their teenage children in what might be described as "locker room" talk. In this situation, they confide the specifics of their own sexual behavior when they were adolescents, often making a joke about it. This approach not only diminishes the gravity of decisions related to sexual behavior, but it also violates that important parent/child boundary by treating our children like our peers. When we make light of these decisions, we also make it harder for adolescents who are already wrestling with their own insecurity to ask serious questions, for fear that they may be ridiculed or that their questions may not be taken seriously.

To address sexual behavior and sexuality effectively, we must first become knowledgeable about the dangers ourselves. In our lifetimes, there have been dramatic changes in the nature and severity of sexually transmitted diseases. In order for us to be fully helpful to our children, we need to first educate ourselves about the current realities. We must know the truth about sexually transmitted diseases and their prevention as well as pregnancy and its prevention. It is not effective to overstate or attempt to use "scare" tactics to discourage sexual behavior. We must stick with the truth, it's frightening enough. To do otherwise will affect our credibility and cause our children to discount our viewpoint.

Homosexuality

Parents must also come to terms with the complex issue of homosexuality. While this issue elicits strong feelings for many of us, there is little evidence that adolescents make a conscious choice to become homosexual. Instead, it currently appears that other factors, not fully understood, affect this preference. Of the adult homosexuals with whom we have worked, not one has ever indicated that he or she "chose" this orientation rather than "becoming" heterosexual. In each case, they talk about a growing awareness that "they were different" and that they became aware of this difference during their adolescence.

Neither religious values nor parents' determination have, in our experience, proven to be an effective deterrent to homosexual behavior. Homosexuality appears to simply be a part of one's sexual identity and we, as parents, need to understand and accept this. Unfortunately, when parents are unable to understand a child's homosexual orientation, unnecessary estrangement and often depression result. Societal rejection of homosexuality has been a significant factor in a large number of adolescent suicide attempts. Because of the complexity of this issue in our society, parents who find themselves faced with this issue may wish to seek outside help or support.

To be an effective guide for adolescents when it comes to their sexuality and sexual behavior, we return to the five tools introduced earlier—listening, expressing feelings, valuing, modeling, and letting go. These tools will lay the groundwork for open communication about one of the most critical issues facing adolescents today.

Listen

Listening with regard to sexual issues means to allow ourselves to hear and understand our children's perspective. This may mean asking questions, then listening and clarifying their responses. Clarifying their responses does not mean to subtlely reflect our own feelings! It simply means asking questions that allow us to fully understand how they see things.

An especially effective question to ask a young adolescent is: "When do you think it is appropriate to become sexually involved in a relationship?" This question and our ability to listen to their answer will help them see us as a credible resource for future questions if they so choose. If we, however, turn this question into a lecture, we will likely shut the door on future conversations. Again, this doesn't mean that we don't express our viewpoint. The best way to do this, however, is to listen first and clarify their perspective, then ask if they would like to hear ours. In most cases, this increases the likelihood that they will choose to listen to us, permitting us to communicate our own values and beliefs without debating or scolding.

Value

In the area of sexuality, honesty and assertive decisions are critical. If we want our teenagers to be good decision-makers, we must tell them when they make good decisions. If we want them to be trustworthy, we must notice it and tell them when they are. Valuing is this simple.

Good parents recognize the qualities that we know will serve our children well in making the right decisions. Remember every time we attribute a quality to our sons and daughters that is positive, it is like putting a label around their neck. They will proudly wear it and act in that manner. The same is true for negative labels, so we must be careful to avoid these.

Finally, it is essential that we be honest. If we label a child as trustworthy when they aren't, our feedback will be seen as dishonest and we lose credibility. If a child is dishonest, we must acknowledge this behavior in this situation by saying "that was dishonest." Notice, however, that we avoid saying "you *are* dishonest" or "you *are* a liar." These statements are shaming and label the child not the behavior.

In the context of sexual decisions, we need to look for opportunities to reinforce healthy characteristics and qualities which we can value explicitly. Of the hundreds of teenagers with whom we have worked, those who have made poor decisions sexually have consistently been those young people who have not seen themselves as valuable! Countless young women each year become pregnant, not because of sexual ignorance, but driven by the need for someone (a child) who will love them unconditionally. Others allow themselves to be used sexually in an attempt gain peer acceptance. Still others, both male and female, become sexually active because they equate sexual activity with adult status (a message promoted frequently by our media and culture).

In each of these cases, the conclusion is obvious. These decisions are made in a vain attempt to increase the teenager's *value,* to themselves or to others. By teaching our children they are valuable, we go a long way toward preventing poor decisions motivated by an attempt to fill an emptiness so many young people seem to experience today.

Model

Modeling in this situation means letting our children know what has contributed to our sexual decisions. To assist parents with this, we have provided a list of behaviors, a suggestion of when such behaviors are appropriate as well as the risks associated with these behaviors. (see Appendix). As these are clearly determined by personal values, we have not intended this to be an authoritative list, but rather a starting point for parents to use in articulating their own position. We suggest that parents review this list, modify it to fit their own values and beliefs, and then discuss these issues with their children in their own way. No matter how we choose to address these issues, it is important that we do so. If we don't, MTV will!

Express Your Feelings

This strategy is a critical one for parents struggling with this issue. Telling our sons and daughters about our fears or concerns will help them understand our perspective and be more considerate of our wishes. This must be done, however, as a simple statement of our feelings and not as a tool to trigger guilt or shame. If it is a manipulation, it will cause resentment and block future communication. If, however, we state that we worry about the decisions they face without making it their additional responsibility to reduce our anxiety, we are being honest with them and will likely earn their respect.

The following example demonstrates a direct expression of feelings:

> *"I feel scared about the pressure to be sexually active which I know you may face once you are dating. Sometimes I know it can seem almost like an obligation, or something you feel you owe somebody."* This expresses a legitimate fear and acts to open communication about the issue.

In contrast, the following is a manipulative statement:

> *"I hope you understand how upset it would make me if you ever got involved sexually before marriage."* This makes the adolescent responsible for our feelings and puts the focus on making us happy rather than the issue of appropriate sexual involvement. It almost certainly discourages further discussion.

Let Go

The final and perhaps most difficult act for any parent is accepting the fact that, ultimately, we cannot make the crucial decisions for our children. They will make their own decisions, just as we made ours, and we are every bit as powerless when this happens as our own parents were. This is why we must work to keep communication open and to assure our children of their own intrinsic worth. In the end, this is the very best we can do. When our children make mistakes, we are left to love them anyway. They need us even more then.

SIX

Dysfunctions of Adolescence

As our children approach adolescence, every parent fears losing control of their child. There are some critical dangers that threaten our children's healthy growth and even their lives as they reach adolescence. The most frequent of these are substance abuse, depression and eating disorders. Each of these represents a significant dysfunction in the two major tasks of adolescence: establishing an identity and gaining independence. Accidents, suicides and homicides are the three leading causes of adolescent deaths. Substance abuse, depression, and eating disorders are among the most significant contributing factors in each of these areas.

Think about the advertisements that promote the use of alcohol. They feature "beautiful people" doing fun things without any suggestion of harmful consequences. They do not feature middle aged men with beer guts screaming at their wives and children. Nor do they feature women looking gaunt and frail after years of abusing their bodies. They absolutely never portray drunken teenagers taking reckless chances, destroying themselves, their friends, and their families, physically and emotionally. These ads speak directly to adolescents. Adolescents are preoccupied with friends, personal appearance, and having fun. They fail to see negative consequences as likely or even realistic. By deliberately targeting the teenage market, alcohol producers guarantee themselves long-term customers. Adolescents get the impression that alcohol is the ticket to "instant adulthood" (independence) and that they will be seen as "beautiful people" (identity). So, the question for loving parents is: How can we prevent children from becoming harmfully involved with alcohol and other drugs? Or, if they do, what can we do to intervene?

Substance Abuse

Among parents' most common fears is the influence of mood altering chemicals like alcohol and marijuana. There is no guaranteed way to protect an adolescent from the hazards of drug use. However, there are ways in which parents can significantly reduce the risk that their children will become harmfully involved with alcohol and other drugs. Additionally, there are a number of resources available to parents to assist them in addressing substance abuse and in intervening should a child become harmfully involved.

What can parents do about this? The time to speak to your child about drug and alcohol use is *not* when they are adolescents. They need to hear about it as early as they can understand the message.

Our attitudes are formed well in advance of adolescence. Those messages which we give our children when they are younger meet with less resistance and are incorporated more deeply than those we attempt to initiate during adolescence. We all realize how much young children mimic their parents' attitudes and beliefs while adolescents rebel against them. So helping them form these beliefs from a young age will enable them to make intelligent and safe decisions when they reach adolescence and help them avoid making danger-ous decisions in later attempts to assert their independence.

While prevention programs offered through the schools are helpful, they are not enough by themselves. Such programs have been demonstrated to be valuable, but parents still need to take the time to be clear about their values and beliefs. Studies have shown that children who choose not to use alcohol or other drugs as adolescents do so because their parents have given them a clear message that this behavior is unacceptable and that there will be sanctions.

Let's look at some of the things parents often say and the messages that are really communicated!

> *"I'd rather that they drink at home than at someone else's house where they may end up having to drive home" Translation:* **"It's OK to drink."**

> *"All kids drink. I did. So I can't see making a big deal about it. I just tell them to use good judgment." Translation:* **"It's OK to use something that im-pairs your judgment, just use good judgment."**

> *"I know my kids drink and have tried marijuana, but they're just experimenting." Translation:* **"It's OK to use as long as you say you're just experiment-ing."** *(Note: An experiment is over when the results are known. Therefore, when a young person uses and realizes that use alters their mood, they are no longer experimenting. They know the results and are now applying them.)*

"I drank as a kid and it didn't effect me at all. I just don't want them using drugs." Translation: **"It's OK to use alcohol (a drug) but don't use drugs."** *(Note: Since it's not always easy to observe someone who's under the influence of other drugs, it's not very likely that this argument will deter an adolescent.)*

Most of these statements reflect our own discomfort with taking a strong position. They are ultimately excuses for substance use. Another dangerous position is that occasional use is acceptable as long as our children don't become addicted. While alcoholism and drug addiction are certainly a concern, *the majority of negative consequences suffered by young people result from drug impairment*, regardless of whether this impairment results from addiction or simply use.

The truth is that all drugs (including alcohol) alter our moods and perception artificially. While impaired functioning is dangerous for any of us, it is particularly dangerous for teenagers. First of all, since teenagers are still developing physically, emotionally, and intellectually, the impact of drugs on their systems is significantly greater. Studies have shown that adolescents are prone to become dependent upon drugs more readily than adults, and that their physical systems are impacted more significantly than adults because of the changing chemistry of young bodies.

Adolescents are far less experienced than adults in every arena of their lives. This means that they are just learning the skills required to drive a car in traffic and to establish healthy relationships with others. Both of these demand critical judgment and appropriate restraint! Police and coroners' reports testify painfully to the impact of drug use on young drivers. Each year, statistics tell the same sad story. The vast majority of all young people killed or injured in traffic accidents are a direct result of a driver or drivers who were under the influence of alcohol or other drugs.

Young women and men who use chemicals often become sexually involved prematurely. Many of these young people experience overwhelming shame when they realize that they have engaged in behavior which violates their own personal values. Should these young people become chemically dependent, the additional burden of sexual shame often makes their recovery far more difficult.

We strongly believe that the only safe message for parents to give their children is that any use of alcohol or other drugs is unacceptable! Evidence supports the fact that the earlier a person uses, the more likely they are to become chemically dependent.

It also appears that healthy maturation comes to a halt when young people begin to rely on drugs for good feelings and to relieve anxiety. This pattern, which Dr. David Logan and Ron Harrison introduced to us as the "maturational arrest syndrome", often results in what Nic has called "a 13-year-old in an 18-year-old suit." They may look like an adult and have adult responsibilities, but are unable to respond in a mature adult manner. This pattern occurs because when their peers were growing up and learning how to apply their skills and solve life's problems, these children came to rely on alcohol and other drugs to merely escape the discomfort the rest of us face when we encounter problems. The result is that they have not matured, or learned from their mistakes.

What tells parents that we need to be concerned? Alcohol and other drugs possess a lure for teenagers which no other activity can match. Jim Crowley, founder of Community Intervention, Inc., observed that "they make you feel good and it works every time. Sports, church, even your best girlfriend can't do that!" Anything this seductive will almost surely trigger changes in attitude and behavior which become evident long before substance abuse itself is visible. For instance, a young person involved in the use of mood-altering chemicals will begin to change interests and friends, and may suffer a decline in performance in school and other activities. We often advise parents that "you don't have to see a kid using to see a using kid."

Look at the following examples:

Holly has always enjoyed playing soccer. This year, however, she decided that she didn't want to join the team. Her reason is that she doesn't have the time.

There are a lot of "Holly's" who make this decision without any problem and who certainly don't have a substance abuse problem. However, if Holly's concern is that she doesn't have the time to do this, the logical question is "what do you need the time for?" For some it will be studies and this will be evident by their behavior. For Holly's who are using drugs or alcohol, they will become more involved with friends and will often fail to be where they said they were going to be. Their desire or need to use drugs will create the need for more unsupervised time.

Jeremy has recently quit hanging around with most of his childhood friends. They are all good students who are actively involved in school activities. Instead, he has chosen to associate with students who are creating problems in school. When asked about his new friends, he states "they accept me for who I am."

Changing friends is as normal in adolescence as finding a new haircut to make your parents crazy. However, when a young person changes friends and changes their image too, it is time to take notice. Even this is not necessarily a clear message that substances are involved, but it may signal a change in self-esteem. We tend to hang around people who feel similarly about themselves. When it is known or expected that these "new" friends use drugs, then it is a virtual certainty that Jeremy is involved too. Kids who don't use rarely choose to associate with friends who do. When Jeremy says that his new friends "accept me for who I am", the unspoken tag line may well be "and I ain't much." Low self-esteem creates natural candidates for substance use.

> *Wendy has always been an "A-" student. In the last six months, however, her grades have dropped sharply. Now earning "C's", she has also lost interest in school. Her earlier goal of attending college and getting a professional job following graduation has also vanished. While her grades have apparently dropped because of her lack of motivation and failure to do assignments, the question is "why?" and "why now?"*

When there is a drop in performance, it is necessary to examine the causes. It doesn't necessarily relate to substance use, however this is frequently the cause. To be certain, examine all the probable causes first. Is there an academic problem that is causing this? Is there a personal problem that is interfering with her ability to concentrate or affecting her motivation? What else has changed since her grades began dropping? When these answers don't suggest a conclusive answer, it is time to consider that Wendy may have begun to use chemicals and thus school has become less important. Remember that nothing can compete with something that "makes you feel good and works every time."

> *Rick came home the other night smelling of alcohol. His parents confronted him, asking him what had been happening. Rick became defensive, saying he was "just with some friends and had a beer. What's the big deal?" His parents have seen no evidence of substance use in the past and this is the first time they've seen him under the influence.*

Rick may or may not be chemically dependent. That, however, is not the issue. What is undeniable is that he is using. His bluster is designed to back his parents off and minimize his use. It has been observed by treatment professionals that adolescents use for approximately *two years* before their parents observe the use or its effects directly. It is a mistake to assume that Rick is experimenting. He needs to be assessed immediately if he is allowing his use to be witnessed by his parents.

> *Rob comes home with a shirt advertising a popular brand of beer. He wears it to school and begins to collect others that carry a similar message glorifying alcohol use.*

Although Rob's choice of shirts doesn't necessarily say he is using, it does say he wants to be seen that way. This is an opportunity for his parents to sit down with him and discuss why he wishes to be seen this way and possible consequences if he wears this type of clothing. Specifically, how will it limit him? If Rob's choice of clothing corresponds with other changes, like a change in friends and a change in performance, it is likely he is using, too.

None of these indicators by themselves (with the obvious exception of observed use) is automatically indicative of substance use or abuse. However, when a cluster of symptoms like these appear, it is time to take notice and seek an assessment from a qualified professional. *Substance use should never be minimized or ignored.* It only takes one decision while impaired to cost the life of your child or someone else's.

So what should parents do if they are concerned? These are our strong recommendations:

Don't keep secrets!

We can't help our child if we don't know what's going on, and aren't willing to find out! You have probably heard it said that "None of us is as smart as all of us." In order to get the necessary facts and observations we need to come to an informed decision, and to provide accurate information to an outside professional, we must be open to the concerns of others. Toward this end, school staff, friends, and other family members need to be invited to share their concerns and observations with us. Under circumstances like these, it is tempting for parents to withhold their concerns, or to share only half-truths, for fear of being seen as bad parents.

For too long, our culture has misunderstood substance abuse and addiction as a shameful behavior of choice, when the overwhelming evidence continues to support the fact that addiction is in fact a disease. When we yield to old stereotypes or attitudes and keep secrets, parents too often allow a treatable problem to become a fatal one.

Learn about the signs of substance abuse

In reading this book, you may be beginning this process. Pick your resources wisely, however. People, like the authors of this book, who have actually worked with substance abusing adolescents and treated ones who were chemically dependent will best understand the signs, symptoms, and appropriate responses. It is also essential you understand chemical dependence as a disease in case it becomes something you must confront.

Ask for help and support

If you have concerns, look for other parents who have dealt with a child's substance abuse or dependence themselves and seek their assistance. Organizations such as Families Anonymous and Tough Love are often good places to meet parents who have faced these same issues. These parents are more than willing to share their experiences and strategies with others, and can assist you in the difficult process of confronting your child effectively. In addition, these parents will be familiar with outside agencies and community resources in your area.

The greatest challenge for parents of children who are harmfully involved with drugs is to avoid what professionals refer to as *enabling*. In simple terms, "enabling" means protecting someone from the natural consequences of self-defeating behavior. When loving parents attempt to protect their children from painful consequences by blaming others, conspiring to keep secrets, or simply denying the painful facts, they only allow them to continue using. Most of us require outside assistance and support in order to maintain a healthy perspective and to do the difficult things we must if we wish to truly assist our children under these circumstances.

Be willing to look at your own use of alcohol and other drugs as well as your family history

As we have already stated, alcoholism and drug addiction are widely recognized today as illnesses, and are defined as such by the American Medical Association. We also know that a predisposition for this illness is transmitted genetically. For this reason, caring parents need to determine honestly the degree to which this illness exists in our own family, both currently and in the past.   For obvious reasons, parents who abuse substances or are alcoholic themselves will be unable to address this issue openly or honestly. They don't see it as a problem, and can't allow themselves to! Such parents will need assistance in recognizing this issue and will almost certainly have to address their own use in order to assist their child. Recognizing and admitting that addiction exists in our own family will allow us to talk to our children and to inform them at an early age about the heightened risk they face if they use.

Finally, be clear about one thing! Adolescents who are abusing substances are frightening. They don't appear to care about anyone or anything and are often completely out of touch with their own feelings. We may take some comfort from the knowledge that beneath their menacing defenses, they are actually frightened, sad, and ashamed. In times like these, they need our help more than at any other time. With appropriate intervention and treatment, they become wonderful, mature and loving children. To better understand this process, listen to our audiotape, *The Road Home,* which includes comments from parents and kids who've successfully weathered this storm.

Depression

Depression is not easy to diagnose in adolescents because of the fact that mood swings are so much a part of normal adolescent development. However, depression does occur for a percentage of adolescents and needs to be addressed in these cases. In order to clarify the issue of depression and how to respond, we have divided it into four categories. It is important to note that the descriptions given here are meant to help guide your actions but are not intended as the basis for a diagnosis.

If you see signs of depression in your child, it is essential that you seek the assistance of a trained psychotherapist who is familiar with adolescents in order to make an accurate diagnosis and prescribe treatment if it is necessary. Adolescent depression often leads to suicide attempts or extreme risk-taking behaviors which can be harmful even if not fatal. Be aware of signs and symptoms and seek outside help if you have any such concerns.

The four divisions which we have described here are considered by experts to be different forms of depression. These categories include: normal moodiness, reactive depression, chronic mild depression, and major depression.

Normal Moodiness

This is what we all see in adolescents from time to time. It is transient and situational. For instance, when your son or daughter fights with a friend or gets a bad grade on a test, they may seem sad and distant. Typically this passes and as the circumstances improve they become happier and more relaxed. The best thing parents can probably do in these situations is to allow for their children's feelings, without trying to coax them out of them. Attempts to "cheer them up" or to coax them out of these feelings may be seen as discounting their feelings. Additionally, this approach is rarely effective.

Experts suggest that it is more helpful to recognize our children's feelings ("you seem sad") and then listen to what happened without judging, simply trying to understand their perspective. Showing a genuine interest in what happened without judging, directing or scolding will open communication and let them own and eventually discover the solution to their problem.

In most cases, this provides the opportunity for them to slowly modify their mood and begin feeling better. If this dark mood doesn't change in a few days or seems to be getting worse, it is time to consult someone for direction. You may want to begin with a school social worker or counselor. If they can't help, then look for a therapist specializing in adolescents.

Reactive Depression

This type of depression is more serious. It results from a trauma and can have profound effects on a child if he or she isn't able to move through it. Unlike the more normal moodiness described above, this type of depression has more dramatic effects. There is also a specific event which triggers it. The significance of this event, usually a loss of some kind, is much greater in the eyes of the adolescent. We must remember that although the scope of this event may not appear as significant to us, the important thing is the power this event holds for our child. We may, for instance, not believe that a school friend moving away is devastating, but this may trigger intense feelings of loneliness or abandonment for our teenage child.

While it is natural for all of us, especially adolescents who experience changes intently, to be "derailed" by any loss, it is also natural for us to adjust over time and deal with such losses. If our children's sadness over any serious loss, whether it be a death, someone moving, a serious injury or illness, or something else traumatic, doesn't show signs of diminishing over a short period of time, then it becomes appropriate for us to become concerned.

Any depression can lead to extreme action if the person's thinking becomes sufficiently distorted. In cases of loss or abandonment, we should take particular note of any indication that our child may be thinking about suicide. Remember that for adolescents, death is such an abstract concept, that they are often inclined to view a personal crisis as much greater than death itself. It's almost as though they don't fully grasp the finality of death, but see it as merely an immediate solution to a traumatic problem. For exactly this reason, we often find ourselves coaching the young people with whom we work to reframe suicide as a "permanent solution to a temporary problem."

Other signs that a reactive depression be growing to something more serious are the avoidance of friends, an inability to concentrate, and generally not feeling good about themselves. Such decreasing self-esteem may appear as loss of interest in things that were previously of great importance, such as dress, academic performance, extra-curricular activities, etc.

Appropriate parental response to reactive depression is much the same as it is for normal moodiness, except that a young person who is experiencing this type of depression is less likely to respond to empathic listening, at least on the initial attempt. Usually short-term therapy is needed to help an adolescent over the hump and to begin feeling focused and in control once again. If your son or daughter mentions or even begins alluding to suicide, be assertive in engaging your child in discussion about this. They may very well be asking for help and feel they need to escalate their pleas to be heard.

There are far too many teenage suicides each year that occur because early signs were ignored or discounted. In these cases, the young people didn't so much wish to end their lives as to have their concerns taken seriously. In most cases, they left clues so they would be stopped before attempting suicide. Experts in the field repeatedly advise that no one ever take a suicide threat lightly! In some situations, they may merely be immature pleas for attention, but one way to stop such behavior is a quick trip to the emergency room for a consultation with a psychiatrist. This sends the clear message to our son or daughter that we love them deeply and will respond to this type of threat seriously and immediately.

Because the threat of suicide is such an important issue when we are dealing with adolescents, parents should be aware of the following signs:

- Any sudden or unexplained happiness or relaxed appearance following a prolonged depression *(This often reflects that the individual has come to a personal decision to take their life and has accepted the consequences.)*
- Talking about suicide *(Listen and respond with concern. Ask for more information and seek professional assistance.)*

- Giving away possessions
  *(Again, this behavior often precedes a suicide attempt.
  The victim is taking care of "unfinished business.")*
- A preoccupation with death in music, art work
  and/or writing
- Sudden lack of academic performance or loss of
  commitment to other previous interests
- Changes in eating and/or sleep habits
- Excessive crying or teariness
- Taking unnecessary risks
- Use of alcohol and/or other drugs
- Inability to concentrate
- Previous suicidal gestures

While no single symptom is necessarily indicative of an impending suicide attempt, we would rather over-react and be wrong than fail to react and be wrong! Remember, when we express concern, the worst that can happen is that we demonstrate our love for our child and send the message that we won't ignore their behavior. Should a cluster of these symptoms appear, parents must be prepared to act quickly and decisively.

Every parent should know the local suicide hotline number or a counseling service we can contact and be prepared to do so if this becomes a concern. (Just as any parent of a toddler makes sure they have the number of the local poison control center, parents of teenagers should be prepared to address depression and potential suicide overtures.)

Chronic Mild Depression

When a child remains in a morose state in which they appear consistently unhappy and show little resilience, the issue may be chronic mild depression. This and the next category, major depression, may have biochemical links. Unfortunately, parents often overlook this type of depression because of its more "chronic" nature—"its just the way he/she *is!*" For this reason, the suggestion to explore this possibility may well come first from outside the family, often from a concerned friend or a school counselor or teacher. They may report that the young person is difficult to motivate, and doesn't seem to see any reason to try things. A pattern of failure frequently begins to emerge, in many cases the result of our child "giving up" too easily or attempting things that "guarantee" failure. Perhaps the most significant distinction between chronic mild depression and major depression is the fact that children suffering from chronic mild depression seem to be happy from time to time, even though it rarely lasts very long.

Adolescents who suffer from chronic mild depression need professional assistance. Sadly, some parents are reluctant to hear this and resist intervention. We often hear parents who are resistant to the idea that their son or daughter could be seriously depressed because they discount this behavior as purely manipulative. Others simply get too far ahead of themselves and choose not to explore this because of a fear that they may be asked to put their child on some form of medication. Such resistance, as in many of the situations we have discussed, often proves disastrous.

We can be the most helpful to our children when we are able to drop our defenses and listen openly to outside suggestions. The feedback parents receive from outside sources is generally intended only to be helpful and not as an attack on our parenting.

Once you select a therapist who has experience treating depressed adolescents, recognize that medication may be prescribed in order to help the child recover a full range of emotions and experience the security and happiness others take for granted. However, it is best to proceed with this cautiously. Most professionals who work with adolescents will treat them with psychotherapy for a period of time to determine if the problem is situational or possibly biochemical. Since adolescence is such a traumatic time characterized by many changes, this approach makes a great deal of sense. In contrast, the same symptoms in adults may be treated with medication earlier.

Major Depression

The final and most serious category of depression is defined as major depression. Like chronic mild depression, it doesn't appear suddenly in response to an event but rather appears as an ongoing element of our child's personality. These children appear sad and/or unable to express any emotion most of the time. Symptoms of major depression include the following:

- Loss of interest in almost everything
- Feeling unloved, lonely, worthless
- Constant boredom/apathy
- Loss of pleasure
- Suicidal thoughts, acts
- Poor concentration

- Trouble with memory
- Social withdrawal
- Diminished school performance
- Running away
- Difficulty sleeping
- Tired when awake
- Loss of appetite

These symptoms are more pronounced in those suffering major depression. Family history is also a significant factor in both chronic mild depression and major depression. There is substantial evidence of a genetic predisposition toward depression. When we know that a parent, uncle, aunt, grandparent or other close relative has suffered from these symptoms, attempted suicide, or been treated for depression, there is an increased likelihood that an adolescent may be experiencing biochemical depression.

Major depression is more likely to require medication, as well as psychotherapy or even temporary hospitalization. As with other forms of depression, parents should be aware of the warning signs for suicide and respond to them assertively.

A Final Note to Parents of Depressed Adolescents

As with substance abuse, it can be frightening for parents who must contend with adolescent depression or possible suicide attempts. To keep our perspective under such trying conditions, we are all well-advised to seek out and utilize support from others. Every community has resources ranging from school counselors and specialists, trained professionals, support groups, and clergy to friends, neighbors, and family members. When we try to deal with these issues alone, we often feel overwhelmed and are more susceptible to making poor decisions. In our efforts to provide support for our children, we shouldn't forget our own need for support.

Eating Disorders

Jamie is an outstanding student. She works extremely hard, earns high grades and stays active in a variety of activities. She's also very concerned about her diet and exercises compulsively. She wears oversized clothing which hides her true body shape. Jamie is slowly killing herself.

Michael is seemingly a happy, well adjusted young man. He doesn't take many things seriously. His classmates like him and enjoy his sense of humor. When Michael is alone, however, he is not nearly as happy. He is also excessively overweight. In fact, he is preoccupied with eating. His counselor once confronted him about his perpetual smile, asking "what would happen if you quit smiling?". Michael was stunned when tears came to his eyes. Michael is also slowly killing himself.

Dawn is a cheerleader and a feisty young lady. She is intelligent, but doesn't always work to her potential. She is fun-loving, but can also be moody. She seems to be concerned about her weight and is secretive

*about her eating habits. She often disappears after
meals, both at home and at school. She is evasive
about where she goes at these times. Her weight
seems to fluctuate dramatically. She too is slowly
killing herself.*

It may seem melodramatic to refer to these hypotheti-
cal young people as "killing themselves" because of their eating disorders, but if these disorders are left untreated, that is
exactly what may happen. In the meantime, we have some
miserable adolescents who may appear to the outside world
as well-adjusted and even successful.

What causes these eating disorders? Why does one
child end up anorexic and another become an overeater?
What can be done about it? All these questions require experts to answer them fully, but in the interest of helping parents who may have to start addressing the issue, we will provide some basic information here.

Family Issues

Families in which eating disorders occur share some
common characteristics. One obvious characteristic is a preoccupation with food. When the issue is anorexia (self-starva-
tion) or bulimia (binge eating and purging), the focus is often
on being thin and eating low-calorie foods. Young women
who become anorexic sometimes begin by being a little overweight and enduring some ridicule from their friends and/or
family. This ridicule may be as subtle as "you would look so
much nicer if you were 15 pounds thinner." Comments like
this can be devastating to a developing adolescent.

In cases of obesity (overeating), food is often used as a

reward or a comfort. A young child who has a bad day expects to be given cookies when he comes home. He does well on a task and is given a treat for a reward. Food often becomes the primary means of addressing difficult feelings or a symbol of celebration.

Control is another issue in families in which eating disorders occur. Anorexics often feel that their parents attempt to run every aspect of their lives. The anorexic quickly discovers that the one thing over which she has complete control is her diet. So, being a perfectionist, she works hard, eats little and hides her feelings.

The Media

The power of the media became apparent to Nic when the ads for Rogaine became popular. As a bald man, one who accepted this early and has had a good deal of fun with it, these ads struck home. All of a sudden, there was his image being projected while a voice-over began by commenting in a disgusted tone, "Would you rather look like this?" then, presenting the image of a full head of hair, "or like this?". Suddenly something that was never a problem actually triggered a momentary impulse to feel ashamed.

Now consider the impact that ads have on adolescents. Can you think of any ads that picture women who are not thin and beautiful, or men who aren't trim and athletic? There are very few ads that don't focus on the "beautiful" (hear "thin") people. Ads that appeal to adolescents are notorious for featuring thin models with the "ideal" body type. Imagine what an adolescent feels who is searching for an identity and looks in the mirror and sees something far different from the ideal. It isn't a surprise that dieting becomes a fad even when weight is within normal limits.

How Does This Happen?

For obese adolescents, it is often a family pattern to overeat or to use food as a reward or comfort as we've already noted. Consequently, eating becomes compulsive and weight becomes a problem. With the added weight comes social isolation with the exception of the young people like Michael who choose the "jolly" route to keep friends. These young people still endure hurtful comments and often suffer from low self-esteem. This is the reason that when Michael is asked about what would happen if he quit smiling, he cries. Underneath it all, he's very sad.

Anorexics and bulimics share some characteristics. Both are perfectionists and prone to be high achievers. Both become preoccupied with losing weight. The anorexic addresses this by starving herself, eating little or focusing on a single food that will be all she eats. She experiences hunger but denies herself food. She knows where every inch of fat is on her body and can recite the calories she's eaten today.

The bulimic is also very focused on losing weight. In this case, however, she (or he) handles it differently. Unlike the anorexic, the bulimic is less apt to be perceived as the perfect student and school leader. She is apt to be a little more oppositional. She also is more apt to have her perfectionist tendencies cause her to give up early rather that become a workaholic like the anorexic.

Her eating habits are different too. She eats in binges, stuffing herself with food, then feels ashamed and purges herself by either vomiting or perhaps by using laxatives to get rid of the food she just ate before it can be fully metabolized. She carries with her a good deal of shame over her eating habits and keeps them secret from those around her. Her parents may notice a fluctuation in her weight, but generally are unaware that anything is wrong.

Responding to an Eating Disorder

As with substance abuse and depression, parents must first become aware of the signs of an eating disorder. We have included a list of the symptoms compiled from a variety of sources in our appendix. Knowing these signs is only part of the solution, though. As with the other issues we have discussed here, it is critical that families get help. It is rare that an eating disorder can be treated in isolation. Families play a major role in creating the dynamics that set the stage for an eating disorder. Whether this is a focus on eating, being thin, or being in control, successful treatment of an eating disorder requires that the family's role be closely examined and addressed.

With an obese child, dieting should be approached cautiously. It can merely lead to a different eating disorder if the focus becomes weight loss rather than good health. The primary goal of intervention must be to reduce the dependence upon food for emotional reward or security, then establish healthy nutrition and exercise habits. The weight loss will follow unless there is some mitigating physical problem that needs to be addressed. In this sense, losing weight is essentially mathematical. Eat healthy food with less calories, and burn more calories and weight drops. The focus, however, is on establishing healthy habits *not* on losing weight.

Finally, it is important to note that the earlier the treatment the better the chance of full recovery. Anorexia is fatal if allowed to progress unchecked. Bulimia and obesity will create dramatic health problems if they are not treated. Appropriate therapy is a necessity since unhealthy family dynamics and an inability to express feelings directly are at the root of each of these disorders.

SEVEN

When To Call
For Help

The time has come. You know it but have a hard time facing it. There is definitely something wrong. Your gut aches, your heart races. You don't know who to talk to or even if you should. You're confused about how this happened and are afraid of what people might think. You know you need help but don't know where to turn. It is a paralyzing fear that grips you, but you also know that you must do something before it is too late. This is what we feel when we begin to recognize that things are out of control.

Despite everything we know about basic first aid and caring for our children's physical health, we all wind up at the doctor's office or hospital eventually. No matter what we do to protect our children from injury and illness, sooner or later situations occur that require someone with special skills. Likewise, there are times when everything we try to do to assist our adolescents' healthy development seems to fail.

At times like these, the best thing that loving parents can do is to seek the advice of a specialist. Just as we aren't ashamed to seek medical attention, we need to accept the fact that no parent can know it all, all of the time. By reading this book, you are already demonstrating your love and commitment to assisting your adolescents through one of the most difficult times in their life. But no one expects each of us to be an expert in everything. When we have tried all the strategies we know and are still dealing with an unhappy, unsuccessful adolescent, we need to seek outside help.

Once we can openly acknowledge that we need help, the next step in this process is to identify our available resources. School counselors and teachers are often a good source of referrals. Their experience with young people has probably made them familiar with specialists in the area. Any other helping professionals with whom we have a relationship can be valuable resources, such as doctors and ministers. Insurance providers can also provide lists of available specialists in a number of fields. Many businesses also provide EAPs (Employee Assistance Plans). These programs are designed to assist employees and their families with personal problems. All of these resources respect client confidentiality and are usually happy to assist parents in locating a specialist who can help us.

Finally, we need to be aware of another possible pitfall. This is what we refer to as the "client-consumer conflict". As a consumer, we must be assertive and cautious. We want to select the very best service available, and be sure that we are getting the greatest value for our time, effort, and money. This requires that we be critical of service providers and insistent upon our rights. However, in our role as the client, we must also let go of some control and understand that the assistance we need may take us outside of our comfort zone by requiring us to try out new behaviors. If we try to play both roles simultaneously, our guardedness as a consumer may block our own growth as a client, or our openness as a client may allow us to be less than an assertive consumer.

Besides merely being aware of this possible conflict,

the most effective strategy to avoid this dilemma may well be to *begin* as an assertive consumer. Initially, we should question providers thoroughly. We have every right to know how we will be charged for service, how our right to confidentiality will be protected, how our growth will be evaluated, who and when will determine when service should be terminated, and any other questions we need answered as a potential consumer. Once we have asked these questions and gotten answers that we find satisfactory, however, we need to trust the specialist we have chosen and allow ourselves to be vulnerable enough to make necessary changes.

Obviously we can never stop being a consumer, nor should we, but we do need to remember why we came here in the first place. No intelligent customer trusts his car to the first garage he happens to see. On the other hand, there is little point in taking your car into a garage, then telling the mechanic what to do and how to do it. If we knew how, or had the time to do it ourselves, we wouldn't be there in the first place!

A *Final* Note

You have and deserve our deepest respect. Surely there can be no more important job anywhere than that of parenting. Not only have you chosen to help raise our next generation, but by reading material like this, you have also demonstrated a desire to improve your parenting skills. It is our fondest hope that some portion of what you have read here will be of practical help in the difficult job you have undertaken.

Parenting adolescents is frequently confusing, can often be disheartening and is always challenging. However one thing remains certain: they need us more than ever. When they don't want us around or argue with everything we say, it may seem as though we're no longer needed. At these times, we may find ourselves tempted to take a back seat, allowing our hurt feelings to control us. The truth is that they need us just as much now as they did when they were infants. Their needs are just less physical and more emotional.

Adolescents, while they thirst for independence and try on different identities, never take their eyes off their parents.

When they push us away, and we don't take offense
but exhibit understanding, we teach them that we

love them even though they are being difficult. They can feel safe.

When they argue and appear to challenge all that we hold sacred and we listen and attempt to understand their views, we teach them respect. They feel respected and more open to what we have to say.

When we set limits on their behavior and don't bend, we establish boundaries for them and teach them important lessons about consequences in the world. They may feel frustrated, but find security in the knowledge that we care about them.

When we apologize to them for our own mistakes, they learn that we are people with our own feelings and failings. They feel less pressure to be perfect themselves.

When we reach out to hug and kiss them like we did when they were younger without taking offense when they make a face and turn away, we teach them that we will respect their boundaries and that we still love them. They feel respected and loved.

When they try on green hair and we grimace but don't put them down, we teach them that we love them for who they are. They feel safe in looking for a new identity knowing we won't abandon them.

When they try smoking cigarettes and we become upset and forbid them from continuing, we teach them that we will not stand idly by while they hurt themselves. They feel safe and loved even if they are angry with us.

When their inappropriate behavior elicits painful consequences from the other authorities in their lives and we don't interfere, they learn that there are natural consequences in the world and we believe they can handle them. They feel trusted and supported, even when they don't think it's fair.

More than anything else, in spite of appearances, they need us to be parents, not friends! They need our love, structure, and respect. In our classes, when we've asked middle school students who has the greatest influence in their life, believe it or not, they continue to say, "my parents."

With this in mind, we have chosen to close by reminding you once again that of all the big and little things that parents do to help our children grow up to be happy, healthy, and successful, the most important step is the final one—that of letting go! It should come as no surprise to any of us that this is so easy to say and so hard to do. After all, we've spent our entire time as parents supporting, encouraging, and "connecting" with our children. To the degree that we've done this well, we have become incredibly attached to them! And so now, suddenly (or at least it seems sudden), we have come to this point at which their growing independence demands that we step back and give them their freedom.

One day while Rick was counseling a group of teenagers, they demanded to know why their parents were so unwilling to let them have more responsibility and freedom. He paused, then asked them to consider the following situation.

"Imagine that you find a baby bird abandoned after a storm. You take him in and keep him warm. Then you read everything you can find, or ask others questions, to learn how to take care of him. You build a small cage, feed him regularly, and protect him from further harm. As he grows, he becomes attached to you and you to him. And then the day comes when you are told it is time to let him go! You know it's the right thing to do because he was born to be free and deserves to go. Yet you have come to care for him, and realize that he has never learned how to take care of himself in the wild. You worry that he may go hungry or be hurt by a predator. No matter how many small opportunities you've provided for him to venture forth in your own yard, you realize that his final departure is drawing nearer. Can you imagine how you would feel about turning him loose?"

The students sat at rapt attention while Rick created this scene for them. When he was done, several students suggested that they would just keep the bird. One student even blurted out, "After all, he's really mine!" Rick simply smiled at them and innocently asked them to remind him what they were discussing before he got off on this story anyway. As they recalled the original issue, the light dawned! Finally, he added that this was simply a "found" bird, and had only been "parented" for a matter of weeks. When he reminded them that their parents had *chosen* to have them, and had raised them for 14 or 15 years, they began to understand the magnitude of the freedom they were now demanding of their parents.

As parents, we need to remember that letting go of our children as they mature is a painful process, and forgive ourselves when we do so awkwardly or reluctantly. After all these years of protecting, directing, and correcting, the idea of stepping back and "setting them loose" seems so contrary to everything we have practiced. However, we must also remember that this is the most important part of our job. This was never intended to be a life-long career! *Parenting children is a stage in our lives, just as childhood is only a stage in our children's lives!* They were always supposed to become adults, and we were always supposed to let them go when this time came. While they will always remain our "children" in one sense of the word, and though we can never love our children too much, it is possible to protect them too much!

We often conclude our parenting workshops with a story we heard from someone else which puts this aspect of parenting in a powerful light. It seems that one day a scientist who studied insects was in the field and came across the flask-shaped cocoon of a rare and beautiful moth. He cut the twig and took the cocoon back to his laboratory so that he would be able to observe the emergence of this incredible specimen.

After several weeks, he entered his lab one morning and detected a rustling from the cocoon. Excitedly, he placed he cocoon on the examination table and watched intently, eagerly waiting for this rare moth to emerge. Soon the head of the moth protruded from the narrow opening at the top of the flask-shaped cocoon. The scientist watched painfully for over two hours while the moth struggled to force its way through the hard, narrow opening. He began to feel guilty about removing the cocoon from its natural habitat and concluded that the cocoon had probably dried out in the unnatural climate of the laboratory. Taking a sharp scalpel, he carefully made an incision in the opening of the cocoon and gently pried it open to relieve the moth's struggles so it could live.

Sitting back, he now watched as the moth gradually freed itself from the cocoon, dragging a huge, swollen body and long, drooping wings onto the table, where it wriggled about, only to die after several minutes. Sad and confused, the scientist researched this species more carefully. Only then did he learn that the prolonged struggle to force itself through the narrow opening of its unique cocoon was a necessary part of nature's design. It was this struggle that forced the fluid out of the large body and into the wings, allowing them to grow to their full majesty. In sorrow, the scientist realized that his efforts to reduce the moth's struggles had been the reason it failed to survive.

As loving parents, probably the most difficult challenge we confront is that of watching our children struggle. How often we find ourselves tempted to just "fix it" for them. And now during adolescence, when they are finally beginning to "emerge" from the cocoon of childhood and take their place in the world as adults, it often seems that their struggles become even more severe. We can all learn a valuable lesson from that scientist. The kindest (and most difficult) thing we can do now is to stand back and demonstrate our faith in and love for our children by allowing them their struggle, remembering that the struggle will make them stronger and allow them to be successful in finding their own freedom and independence.

"Letting Go"

Appendix

APPENDIX A:
SEX, GROWING UP AND RELATIONSHIPS

Introduction

The following appendix is an attempt to offer parents a guide to discussing some of the more difficult but important issues our children face. It is not meant to be a "recipe" but a guide. The sexual behavior discussed is not intended to be all-inclusive, but to illustrate a progression of behaviors. Obviously, engaging in sexual behaviors of any kind is governed by a value system. Parents need to make these values explicit before their children engage in sexual behavior. How this is done depends on the opportunities available, the comfort level of the parents and the history of communication between parents and their children. However, we believe that parents who postpone such a discussion because of their own discomfort leave the door open for the media, innuendo, and children's peers to replace them as a major influence.

We offer the following guide to parents with the suggestion that you read it carefully, use it if it reflects your own values or revise it so that it does, then find the best way to initiate a discussion with your child about these behaviors.

This appendix includes four sections:

Section 1—*Perspectives on Critical Terms of Adolescence*

This section gives a perspective on three terms that often become "flash points" or points of conflict with adolescents. As stated before, these represent our perspective and should be altered to reflect yours.

Section 2—*Risks and responsibilities of sexual behavior*

This section is the one in which we describe an explicit progression of sexual behaviors (ours) and indicate the risks as well as when each behavior is appropriate. Again, read this, decide if or how you will use it and make it reflect your values and beliefs.

Section 3—*Healthy relationships*

This section is a series of questions that indicate the health of a relationship. It originates from information found in literature about abusive and dysfunctional relationships.

Section 4—*Starting the discussion*

This section gives some ideas for opportunities to open meaningful discussion about the issue of sexual behavior and the values governing it. In this section, we also provide ideas for opening questions to start the discussion.

❧

Section 1: Critical Terms

ABOUT INTIMACY

Intimacy is *not* about sex. Intimacy is about getting to know another person thoroughly. This means knowing how he or she feels about things, how she or he expresses feelings, what his or her strengths and weaknesses are. It also means being safe and accepted for who you are without having to make any "false pretenses". When you are mature enough to be intimate with a person on this basis, then physical intimacy can become a part of the relationship.

ABOUT MATURITY

Maturity is not entirely about age, although age does play a part. Maturity comes when you have experienced enough of the "ups" and "downs" of life to feel truly self-confident. You know your limits or boundaries and will not exceed them. You understand that a true friend will not expect you to do something that makes you feel uncomfortable. You also are clear about your values and make decisions consistent with these values. You are unwilling to sacrifice your self-esteem for anyone else. When you are mature, you can see beyond your immediate needs and be considerate of the other person. When you are mature, true intimacy, both emotional and physical, is possible. Without maturity, neither can happen.

ABOUT GROWING UP

Growing up takes time. You can't rush it. Growing up is not measured by what a person does but by how a person handles him or herself. You become grown up by experiencing life as it happens in ways that are appropriate for your age. Engaging in adult behaviors such as drinking and sexual intercourse do not make a person grown up. Engaging in these behaviors only creates the illusion of being grown up while robbing you of important adolescent experiences essential to becoming a healthy adult.

❧

Section 2: Risks and Responsibilities

DEALING WITH SEXUAL FEELINGS OUTSIDE OF A RELATIONSHIP

Behavior

Masturbation

When it is appropriate

Masturbation is a private behavior. It is an appropriate and normal way to deal with sexual feelings and urges. It is not appropriate to engage in this behavior in a situation where privacy is not assured.

Risks

While masturbation is a typical way to address sexual feelings in adolescence and throughout your life, it becomes a reason for concern if it becomes an obsessive behavior.

DEALING WITH SEXUAL FEELINGS WITHIN A RELATIONSHIP

STAGE I

Behavior

Holding hands

Hugging

Kissing on the cheek

Kissing on the lips with mouth closed

When it is appropriate

This behavior is appropriate when you have had some time to be around the other person and have some idea what they are like. So far you find him or her attractive. Kissing too soon may

signal an impatience to go farther which is not safe with someone you don't know well.

Risks

These behaviors are relatively low-risk, especially if you have
given yourself time to get to know the other person. As mentioned previously, if you move too quickly into this stage, you
may find yourself being pressured to go farther even though
you may not be ready.

STAGE II

Behavior

Open mouth kissing
Petting over clothes

When it is appropriate

It is important that you know that you are with someone you
can trust and who will respect your limits. If you haven't ever
talked about this, you probably should not engage in these behaviors. It is essential to have known the other person for
awhile and seen them experience a variety of emotions. Generally, these behaviors as well as those in the subsequent stages
are not appropriate for middle school students.

Risks

If you engage in these behaviors with someone you do not
know well and, therefore, can't trust completely, you may
again trigger a desire to go further. Petting in the genital area
may cause a person to approach an orgasm which may, in
turn, cause him/her to become aggressive about getting
his/her needs met. She/he may misread you and believe that
you are signaling that you want to go further. You must know
the other person well enough to know that he/she will respect

your wishes. As was stated before, the best precaution is to talk about your limits before you get involved.

STAGE III

Behavior

> Petting under clothes
> Undressing each other
> Mutual masturbation

When it is appropriate

> This behavior should be engaged in only with someone you know well and have been around for a long time. In this case, a long time is more than a few weeks. Trust is paramount when engaging in this behavior because you are making yourself so vulnerable. It is best to have made some commitment to a relationship with the other person.

Risks

> This behavior may lead to an orgasm. If you do not know the other person well, have no commitment to her/him, or cannot totally trust him/her, you are making yourself very vulnerable to unwanted intercourse or date rape. A decision to have intercourse needs to be made weighing all the potential consequences and responsibilities. You should definitely have spoken about your limits before engaging in this behavior.

STAGE IV

Behavior

> Sexual intercourse

When it is appropriate

> This behavior carries with it the possibility of enormous responsibilities and potentially serious consequences. It is best not to

engage in this behavior until you are with someone to whom you have made a lifetime commitment. Since your partner may become the parent to your child, it is essential that you know this person well, can trust her/him and have been in a relationship with him/her for some time.

Risks

The risks are fairly clear. Sexual intercourse can produce children even if birth control is used. Unwanted pregnancies can lead to marriages that are inappropriate or unduly stressed. They can also lead to a decision to terminate the pregnancy. Abortion invariably creates serious emotional consequences. Likewise, it is never easy to give a child up for adoption once it has been carried full term.

A teenage single mother who elects to keep the child will minimally delay her own career development and ability to become independent. She sets herself up to possibly face poverty. She will also sacrifice the social aspects of her school years.

In addition to pregnancy, sexually transmitted diseases are also a danger. If you do not know your partner well, you may be with someone with a promiscuous past who is carrying some STD including AIDS. It is important to remember that you are not only sleeping with this one person but with everyone they have slept with previously as well as all of their previous partners' previous lovers, and so on. Again this is why trust and a lifelong commitment is essential before engaging in this behavior.

᳇

Section 3: Healthy Relationships

A healthy relationship is one in which each person feels good about him/herself. Both are comfortable being together as well as being alone. Both can express a wide range of feelings with each other. Neither feels possessive or jealous of the other. Neither feels a need to "change" the other person in order to make him or her the kind of person they can enjoy. Neither feels a need to control the other person. Within healthy relationships, people do not fear for their safety at any time. Trust is established and not compromised.

Is your relationship healthy? Check it with these questions. (To make this less awkward, the term partner is used to describe the person with whom you have a relationship.) Where concerns become evident, discuss them openly. An unwillingness to discuss them should be seen as a sign of an unhealthy relationship.

Do you feel good about yourself?

Do you feel like your partner is necessary to make your life happy?

Can you express all feelings with your partner without fear of ridicule or abuse? For example, can you express fear, sadness, anger, embarrassment, joy, etc.?

Does your partner accept your limits on sexual behavior?

Are you pressured to engage in behaviors that make you feel uncomfortable? For example, going farther sexually than you'd like, engaging in risky behaviors like skipping school, shoplifting or reckless driving, engaging in drinking, smoking or using drugs, etc.?

Do you believe that your partner feels good about him/herself?

Do you or your partner feel jealous or possessive?

Does your partner resist or resent your accomplishments?

Do you or your partner attempt to change the other person?

Has your partner ever hit you, called you derogatory names or been abusive in other ways?

Do you or your partner engage in self-destructive behaviors such as drinking, using drugs, or smoking?

Do you or your partner try to control who the other person hangs out with?

Do you and your partner share common interests and values?

Section 4: Discussion Starters

Teachable moments: These are times when you and your son or daughter are engaged in a heartfelt, deep, or intimate discussion. When you are modeling intimate communication, practicing good listening skills and getting the results of a warm discussion, it may be time to open this subject if the opportunity presents itself. Open with a open-ended question, however, not a lecture.

Watching TV or a movie: There are parents who forbid their children to watch certain TV shows or movies. This is one approach which, when accompanied by a clear explanation, may work. Such a moment may also provide an opportunity to engage in a discussion, not a lecture, about sexual behavior. To impact on your children's values they must first feel respected.

Other parents use these TV shows or movies as a conduit for revealing their values. For example, watching a movie together that portrays sexual behavior as casual and without consequences provides an excellent opportunity to suggest that this isn't realistic nor does it reflect your values.

Probably the easiest way to engage in this discussion is to begin at the end, so to speak. Since adolescents expect our greatest concern to be with the issue of sexual intercourse, this is a more natural opening. By beginning with a discussion of intercourse and possible consequences, we can more naturally carry this discussion to the sexual behaviors that precede intercourse.

Opening questions:

> *"You're getting to an age when sexual behavior will become an issue. Tell me what you would expect in a rela-*

*tionship before you chose to be sexually involved with
someone."*

Such a question can be followed with other non-judgmental questions
("tell me more"). Then ask if your son or daughter would like your perspective. To many parents' surprise, they often ask for our perspective,
if we have been respectful and listened to them first. If they don't express an interest in our perspective at this point, then we shouldn't
force it on them. This surprises them in turn and leaves them feeling
curious. Almost certainly, another opportunity will present itself and
they will feel that they can trust us because of the respect we have
demonstrated.

Watching a TV show or movie that doesn't reflect your values:

> *"Tell me what message this movie conveys regarding . . .
> (pick one or more depending on the situation) a) the
> treatment of women, b) the presence of sex in a relation-
> ship, c) the treatment of men, or d) the use of obscene or
> profane language."*

After clarifying their response with "tell me more" type of questions,
follow this again with a question like "Do you want to know what I
think?" They will be willing to listen if you have listened non-judg-
mentally first.

APPENDIX B:
SIGNS OF SUBSTANCE ABUSE

OBSERVED CHANGES:

- Changing friends—being with others you suspect may use substances
- Changing motivation—losing interest in achieving in school, dropping sports or other activities
- Changing performance in school—declining grades, increased disciplinary referrals, increased absences and tardiness
- Changing relationship with the family—withdrawing from family interaction, anger or aggression toward parents refusal to observe limits or false compliance ("Whatever you say", followed by independent behavior)

DISHONESTY:

- Dishonest about where they are spending their time.
- Dishonest about behavior when confronted
- Stealing money or possessions
- Skipping school or other activities

MENTAL HEALTH:

- Making immature decisions—not showing appropriate maturity
- Extreme mood swings
- Depression

PHYSICAL HEALTH:

- Appearance changes, poor grooming or hygiene
- Signs of smoking cigarettes evident, (deep persistent cough, smell of tobacco)
- Loss of vitality

DISINTEGRATION OF VALUES:

- Engaging in behavior that is opposite of the values they held previously (e.g., being violent, hurtful, profane, prematurely sexual, etc.)
- Hurtful towards parents and siblings—pushing them away
- Not engaging in church or other similar activities
- Wearing clothing that glorifies the use of alcohol or other drugs

PRESENCE OF SUBSTANCES:

- Observed under the influence
- Paraphernalia found including cigarettes, lighters, cigarette papers, "bongs", beer cans, liquor bottles, etc.

Note: No one of these behaviors alone is symptomatic of a substance abuse problem. However, a combination of these symptoms indicates a potential problem. If it feels like something is wrong and several of these behaviors are evident, see a professional who specializes in adolescents and who understands and does not excuse adolescent substance use.

APPENDIX C:
EATING DISORDERS

**DEFINITIONS OF VARIOUS EATING DISORDERS
AFFECTING ADOLESCENTS:**

Anorexia Nervosa—"refusal to maintain body weight over a minimal normal weight for age and height; intense fear of gaining weight or becoming fat, even though underweight; a distorted body image; and amenorrhea (in females)." (Diagnostic and Statistical Manual of Mental Disorders—III—R, 1987, p. 65).

People with this disorder experience themselves as being fat even though they are underweight. They will often wear clothing to hide their actual body shape and will be able to identify exactly where the fat is on their body. They achieve weight loss by reducing food intake substantially, exercising excessively and by purging through self-induced vomiting.

OTHER SYMPTOMS:

- Growth process slows or stops; loss of weight
- Lack of energy, dizziness, light headedness
- Physical symptoms like dull, limp hair which may become thin or fall out; pale grayish skin, brittle nails; appearance of fine dark hair all over body (known as tanugo); loss of menstruation in females, etc.
- Sensitivity to cold temperatures
- Long term physical damage to kidneys, heart, and brain
- Death if it is not treated

EARLY SIGNS:

- Highly perfectionist behavior
- Seen as "model" child
- Withdraws, becomes depressed or in some instances defiant
- Difficulty expressing feelings and thoughts
- Inability to make decisions
- Withdrawal from relationships, may cling to a parent

Bulimia Nervosa—"recurrent episodes of binge eating (rapid consumption of a large amount of food in a discrete period of time); a feeling of lack of control over eating behavior during the eating binges; self-induced vomiting, use of laxatives or diuretics, strict dieting or fasting or vigorous exercise in order to prevent weight gain; and persistent overconcern with body shape and weight." (Diagnostic and Statistical Manual of Mental Disorders—III—R, 1987, p. 67).

This disorder is characterized by binge eating and purging. The binge eating behavior is usually done secretly. Those suffering from this disorder usually feel ashamed and depressed after an episode of binge eating and purging.

OTHER SYMPTOMS:

- Weakness, dizziness, headaches
- Muscle cramps and/or numbness in legs
- Difficulty swallowing or keeping food down
- Swollen and/or infected salivary glands
- Damage to esophagus
- Excessive tooth decay
- Electrolyte imbalance
- Long term effects may include heart damage or failure or colon failure

EARLY WARNING SIGNS:

- Depressed but often more rebellious behavior
- May lose or gain weight; weight fluctuates
- Perfectionist but more likely to not try when challenged than the person suffering from anorexia nervosa
- Self-critical, unable to accept criticism without feeling ashamed
- Difficulty in social interactions, keeps others distant

Note: The above information comes from a variety of sources, including the DSM-III-R, the Michigan Model for School Health Education, information from Dr. Maria Beye, a psychologist specializing in eating disorders, and from our personal experiences working with adolescents suffering from these disorders. It should be used as a tool to help understand what might be happening. If you have concerns, contact a treatment professional in your area who specializes in adolescent eating disorders.

APPENDIX D:
STRATEGIES FOR
STRUCTURING HEALTHY GROWTH

TEACH

- State your expectations and values clearly in a non-shaming manner.
- Use specific examples.
- "Model" desired behavior whenever possible.

AFFIRM

- Be attentive to incremental change.
- Notice responsible behavior.
- Seek opportunities to "value" your child.
- Avoid the temptation to mention shortcomings in valuing statements. (e.g.. "You are so helpful and responsible at home . . . I just wish you did half that well in school!)

SET LIMITS

- Communicate limits and consequences specifically.
- Make sure all limits and consequences are understood well in advance.
- Consider drafting a "home contract" which includes these expectations and onsequences.

- Select consequences which:
  - have perceived value
  - can be easily administered
  - won't become a source of resentment for you
  - are linked to behavior as directly as possible
  - are not shaming in nature

KNOW YOUR OWN LIMITS AND ADDRESS THEM

GET OUTSIDE HELP WHEN:

- behavior appears to be out of control
- a family crisis taps your emotional resources
- there is an abrupt change in behavior
- behavior is dangerous

REFERENCES

Story on Page 14:

> *Chicken Soup for the Soul* (First Edition), Jack Canfield and Mark
> Victor Hansen, ed. Page 103-104, Patricia Fripp: *What You Are Is As
> Important As What You Do*

The family roles alluded to in Chapter 2, page 50, can be found in Claudia
Black's book: *It'll Never Happen to Me!,* published by MAC in Denver in 1981
and in Sharon Wegscheider's book: *Another Chance,* published by Science
and Behavior Books in Palo Alto in 1981.

ADDITIONAL
RESOURCES AVAILABLE

Earnie Larsen's books, tapes, and recovery programs are available through Earnie Larsen Enterprises, 7549 Douglas Drive North, #106, Brooklyn Park, MN 55443, Phone: (800) 635-4780 or (612) 560-4197. A list of his books and services can also be found at his web site: www.earnie.com.

To order a copy of the audiotape produced by Nic and Rick, *The Road Home,* mentioned in this book, send a check for $10.00 to Willow Creek Publishing, 6506 Paul Revere Lane, Canton, MI 48187. This tape is 70 minutes long and includes comments from parents of recovering chemically dependent teenagers as well as the recovering teenagers themselves. It is designed for parents or professionals who are concerned their students or sons and daughters may have a substance abuse problem or who have placed their sons or daughters in treatment. Schools and treatment programs have also purchased these tapes.

ABOUT THE AUTHORS

Authors Nic Cooper and Rick McCoy

Nic and Rick have each spent over 25 years working with adolescents in schools and in treatment settings. Nic began as a high school counselor, developed alternative programs and co-directed them for 13 years in the Plymouth-Canton school district. Rick began his career working in treatment programs for emotionally impaired adolescents. He moved into special education in the public schools. Eventually, he teamed with Nic in developing and running alternative education programs. Both Nic and Rick helped initiate an aftercare program at Growth Works, Inc., in Plymouth, Michigan, working as group and individual therapists for recovering chemically dependent adolescents and their parents.

Nic and Rick also formed a consulting and training business, offering workshops to schools and businesses which addressed issues ranging from chemical dependence to communication and conflict resolution. Their workshops included "How to Help the Kid You'd Like to Strangle", for teachers of at-risk students; "Growing Parents, Growing Kids", a family development workshop for families of adolescents; and the series from which this book evolved, "How to Keep Being a Parent When Your Child Stops Being a Child".

Nic also worked as an adult probation officer, a work detail supervisor for the adult probation department, and a middle school counselor. He is currently an assistant principal at Saline Middle School in Saline, Michigan. He has a B.A. in psychology from Wittenberg University, an M.A. from Western Michigan University in counseling and student personnel, and is currently completing his dissertation for an Ed. D. in educational leadership from Eastern Michigan University.

Rick also directed a summer camp for the Hemophilia Foundation of Michigan for several years. He currently works as a teacher in the high school alternative education program for Plymouth-Canton schools. Rick has a bachelors degree in psychology from Albion College, and a master's degree in special education from Eastern Michigan University. Both are certified social workers in the state of Michigan.

ABOUT THE ILLUSTRATOR

It only seemed natural to us to consider a young person when we were seeking an illustrator for our material. **Kevin Franks** is an 18-year-old student in the Plymouth-Canton School District and has been drawing all of his life. He hopes to attend the Center for Creative Studies in Detroit and is looking forward to a career in art. We are in awe of his ability to take nothing more than our vague descriptions and produce the exact illustrations we had in our minds.